Infotech
English for computer users

Third edition

Teacher's Book

Santiago
Remacha Esteras

PUBLISHED BY THE PRESS SYNDICATE OF THE UNIVERSITY OF CAMBRIDGE
The Pitt Building, Trumpington Street, Cambridge, United Kingdom

CAMBRIDGE UNIVERSITY PRESS
The Edinburgh Building, Cambridge CB2 2RU, UK
40 West 20th Street, New York, NY 10011–4211, USA
477 Williamstown Road, Port Melbourne, VIC 3207, Australia
Ruiz de Alarcón 13, 28014 Madrid, Spain
Dock House, The Waterfront, Cape Town 8001, South Africa

www.cambridge.org
www.cambridge.org/elt/infotech

© Cambridge University Press 1993, 1999, 2002

It is normally necessary for written permission for copying to be obtained *in advance* from a publisher. The normal requirements are waived here and it is not necessary to write to Cambridge University Press for permission for an individual teacher to make copies for use within his or her own classroom. Only those pages which carry the wording '© Cambridge University Press' may be copied.

First published 1993
Second edition 1999
Third edition 2002
Reprinted 2004

Printed in the United Kingdom at the University Press, Cambridge

ISBN 0 521 75429 1 Teacher's Book
ISBN 0 521 75428 3 Student's Book
ISBN 0 521 75430 5 Audio Cassette
ISBN 0 521 75431 3 Audio CD

Contents

Acknowledgements	iv
Introduction	1

Section 1 Computers today — 3
- **Unit 1** *Computer applications* — 4
- **Unit 2** *Computer essentials* — 8
- **Unit 3** *Inside the system* — 11
- **Unit 4** *Bits and bytes* — 16
- **Unit 5** *Buying a computer* — 20

Section 2 Input/output devices — 23
- **Unit 6** *Type, click and talk!* — 24
- **Unit 7** *Capture your favourite image* — 27
- **Unit 8** *Viewing the output* — 31
- **Unit 9** *Choosing a printer* — 35
- **Unit 10** *I/O devices for the disabled* — 39

Section 3 Storage devices — 42
- **Unit 11** *Magnetic drives* — 43
- **Unit 12** *Optical breakthrough* — 46

Section 4 Basic software — 49
- **Unit 13** *Operating systems* — 50
- **Unit 14** *The graphical user interface* — 53
- **Unit 15** *A walk through word processing* — 56
- **Unit 16** *Spreadsheets* — 59
- **Unit 17** *Databases* — 62
- **Unit 18** *Faces of the Internet* — 65

Section 5 Creative software — 69
- **Unit 19** *Graphics and design* — 70
- **Unit 20** *Desktop publishing* — 73
- **Unit 21** *Web design* — 76
- **Unit 22** *Multimedia* — 79

Section 6 Programming — 83
- **Unit 23** *Program design* — 84
- **Unit 24** *Languages* — 87
- **Unit 25** *The Java revolution* — 91
- **Unit 26** *Jobs in computing* — 94

Section 7 Computers tomorrow — 97
- **Unit 27** *Electronic communications* — 98
- **Unit 28** *Internet issues* — 101
- **Unit 29** *LANs and WANs* — 104
- **Unit 30** *New technologies* — 108

Extra activities — 112

Extra activities: Answer key — 125

Acknowledgements

Unit 8, Task 4: The listening text is adapted from *Understanding Computers* by Nathan Shedroff, J. Sterling Hutto and Ken Fromm, by permission of SYBEX Inc. ISBN number 0-7821-1284-X, Copyright 1993, SYBEX Inc. All rights reserved.

The author gratefully acknowledges the help of Ben Graham in preparing this work for publication.

The author and publishers are grateful to the following photographic sources for permission to reproduce photographs: p9 Nigel Luckhurst; p122 l Image Bank/Nicolas Russell; c,r © Pictor International.

Introduction

1 Who is the book for?

Infotech is an intermediate-level English course for students of computer science and technical English in secondary schools and technical colleges. It aims to help these students to develop a great variety of language skills and to acquire a knowledge of computers *in English*.

Infotech is also suitable for in-house training programmes, and for institutions where English has become a requisite for working with computers. This book is intended to help staff using computers to understand a wide range of texts about information technology.

2 What does this book consist of?

The Student's Book contains:
- 30 units organized into seven sections (each unit provides an average of two hours of work)
- a detailed map of the book
- a Glossary of technical terms
- a list of acronyms and abbreviations.

The Teacher's Book contains:
- unit planning sheets with practical teaching suggestions. Teachers can also use these sheets to make notes about optional materials, learning difficulties and evaluation.
- answer keys to the exercises
- tapescripts for the material on cassette
- technical help where it is required
- extra activities which can be used either for class work or for homework in conjunction with the Student's Book. They can also be used as exercises to test the student's progress.

3 Organization

The material is organized into 'thematic' **sections** which cover a wide variety of topics and styles of presentation. It is based on skills development and communicative tasks.

Each section consists of various **units** based on the same theme. The first page of each section sets the theme and provides the learning objectives.

Most of the units follow a similar pattern:
- A '**pre-task**' to make the texts more accessible and prepare the students for the main task.
- A **main task** which focuses on a particular skill.
- **Language work and vocabulary exercises**. The purpose of these 'enabling activities' is to prepare students for freer practice.
- A **follow-up task**. The aim of this is to provide students with more opportunities for speaking or writing.

Although the overall framework of each unit is largely the same, the variety of tasks makes each unit unique.

4 Skills development

Infotech lays particular emphasis on developing receptive skills – reading and listening – although they are supported by speaking and writing activities.

- The **reading** texts are mostly authentic or adapted from original sources – specialist magazines, computer programs and reference manuals – so they are related to the learner's own experience. The tasks are designed to develop a great variety of reading strategies, such as skimming, scanning, matching texts to pictures, etc. Text analysis is also a relevant feature of this book: students have to look for information, find reference signals, identify cohesion devices or distinguish facts and opinions.
- The **listening** passages include conversations (e.g. buying a computer), interviews, advertisements, descriptions of hardware and software, etc. It can be helpful to start the listening tasks with a pre-listening activity such as pre-teaching vocabulary, 'brainstorming' the topic, etc.

- The **speaking** tasks develop oral skills through quizzes, role plays, information-gap and problem-solving activities.
- The approach to **writing** is based on two assumptions: (i) writing is an interactive process where the writer tries to communicate something to a real or imaginary reader; (ii) the organization of ideas is as important as grammatical accuracy. Consequently, the students are encouraged to write complete, coherent texts. The writing tasks include describing objects and diagrams, making advertisements, summarizing texts and writing letters.

5 Grammar and vocabulary

The **language** tasks revise the major language points necessary at this level. The HELP boxes in the units are designed as a resource which can be used as part of classroom teaching or outside the classroom. The language work concentrates on those grammatical constructions which are typical of technical English (passive forms, imperatives, comparatives and superlatives, discourse markers, etc.). Grammar exercises are contextualized and arise from the linguistic forms that appear in the texts. Sometimes students have to work out the grammar for themselves.

The book lays special emphasis on **vocabulary** acquisition. Here are a few tips about how to deal with it:

- Explain the difference between 'active' and 'passive' vocabulary. Some students are not conscious of this distinction and are very anxious about their lack of active vocabulary. 'Active vocabulary' refers to those lexical items that the student is able to use appropriately in oral and written communication. 'Passive vocabulary' refers to those items that can be recognized and understood during the process of listening and reading. Passive vocabulary is much easier to acquire than active vocabulary at any stage in the learning process.
- Tell your students that they do not need to understand every word, and encourage them to guess the meaning from context. When they meet unknown words it is also very useful to work out what part of speech they are. Word-building exercises and the study of word formation processes (affixation, conversion and compounding) will help them to develop and extend their vocabulary.
- Draw students' attention to the Glossary for help with acronyms and technical terms.
- Train students to use their dictionaries properly. Students should be able to understand the pronunciation guidance, the layout of entries, abbreviations, etc. Occasionally it may be useful to work with a dictionary of computer terms.
- Encourage students to create personal archives of vocabulary. The traditional idea of making bilingual lists of vocabulary can be transferred to the computer. Some students may like to store and organize vocabulary on disk instead of the traditional notebook.

Internet work

The Infotech website at *www.cambridge.org/elt/infotech* provides students with more opportunities to develop their knowledge and language skills through the Internet.

Internet icons at the end of units in the Student's Book indicate two types of activity on the website:

a) *Study online* activities - texts and exercises for students to complete online or for the teacher to print out and use in class.
b) *Web links* activities - tasks based on links to external websites, which have been carefully selected for their interesting topics and accessible language. The teacher may like to set these activities as homework.

The Infotech website is regularly updated to reflect advances in computer technology.

Note

The course does not require a specialist knowledge of computers, but it is advisable for teachers to understand the basic concepts and terminology of each unit. These are explained in the 'Technical help' sections in each unit.

Computers today

Unit		page
1	*Computer applications*	4
2	*Computer essentials*	8
3	*Inside the system*	11
4	*Bits and bytes*	16
5	*Buying a computer*	20

Unit 1 *Computer applications*

Topic	Skills
Different uses of computers	**Listening:** Listening for specific information in short descriptions
Learning objectives	**Reading:** Looking for new uses of computers in a text
To talk and write about computer applications in everyday life	**Speaking:** Discussing what computers can do in particular areas
Language	**Writing:** Summarizing a discussion
Grammar: Present simple passive	**Internet work**
Vocabulary: Computers in education, sports, entertainment, medicine, etc.	(optional) PCs: History and development

Plan

Teacher's activities	*Students' activities*	*Comments*
Section page You may want to point out the learning objectives to your SS.		
1 Match the pictures In **A** to **C** encourage SS to guess the meaning of unknown words from the context. In **D** you may like to write some key language on the board: *Computers are used to …* *They can help us store/make calculations.* You can write SS' answers on the board.	Using the texts and illustrations, SS do **A** to **C**. SS discuss the questions in **D** as a whole class.	This first unit is deliberately less technical than others. It is meant to be a gentle introduction to the book.
2 Listening Play the cassette, pausing after each speaker. Play it again and check answers with the whole class. (You could write the table on the board.)	SS listen and complete the first column of the table. Then they compare answers with a partner. SS listen again and complete the table.	
3 Reading Go round and monitor the activity. Check answers with the whole class.	SS first write a list of computer applications. Then they read the passage and underline any uses that are not in their lists.	
4 Language work: The present simple passive Direct SS' attention to the HELP box. Check answers with the whole class.	SS look at the HELP box and do the exercise individually. Then they check their answers in pairs.	The passive voice is very frequent in technical English.

5 Other applications

A Circulate among the groups and provide vocabulary as the need arises. B Give help with the summaries if necessary. Ask each group to appoint a spokesperson to give an oral report to the class.	Each group discusses the use of computers in one of the four areas. They listen to each other's summaries and ask questions.	Weaker SS may find it difficult to talk about the use of computers in a certain area. Draw their attention to the *Useful words* and *Useful constructions* boxes.

Evaluation of the unit: ....
....

Answer key

1 Match the pictures

A
1 b   2 d   3 a   4 c

B
Using an automatic cash dispenser: a
In education, computers can make all the difference: b
Organizing the Tour de France demands the use of computer technology: d
Controlling air traffic: c

C
1 noun   2 noun   3 verb   4 adjective
5 noun or verb   6 adjective   7 noun or verb
8 verb   9 noun   10 adjective
a 2   b 3   c 6   d 7   e 10   f 8
g 4   h 5   i 1   j 9

2 Listening

See tapescript in panel on page 6 and completed grid on page 7.

3 Reading

Computer uses and applications mentioned in the text include:
  computer-aided design of buildings
  magazine production
  preparation of bills
  operation of telephone network
  making a flight reservation
  making a bank transaction
  calculators
  car's electronic ignition
  timer in microwave
  programmer in TV
  management of large collections of data
  computer games.

4 Language work: The present simple passive

1 are connected
2 are known
3 are typeset
4 is processed
5 is used
6 is supported
7 are coordinated
8 is held

5 Other applications

A
Possible answers
- *Formula 1:* Computers are used to design and construct racing cars. Computers help engineers to design the car body and the mechanical parts. During races, a lot of microprocessors control the electronic components of the car and monitor the engine speed, temperature and other vital information.
- *Entertainment:* People use computers to play all kinds of computer games: chess, adventure games, simulation games, etc. Fortunately,

Tapescript

1. I write music mainly for videos and plays. I work on a keyboard connected to a computer. I use the computer in *two* ways really: first of all, to record what I play on the keyboard, in other words to store what I play on the keyboard. Secondly, the computer controls the sounds I can make with the different synthesizers I have here. I can use it to get different kinds of sounds from the synthesizers. The computer is the link between the keyboard which I play and the synthesizers which produce the sounds.

2. I use my computer to do the usual office things like write memos, letters, faxes and so on, but the thing which I find really useful is electronic mail. We're an international company and we have offices all over the world. We're linked up to all of them by e-mail. With e-mail I can communicate with the offices around the world very efficiently. It's really changed my life.

3. Well, I use computers for almost every aspect of my job. I use them to design electrical installations and lighting systems: for example the program will tell you how much lighting you need for a particular room, or how much cable you need, and it will show where the cable should go. I also use the computer to make drawings and to keep records. We have to test our installations every five years and the information is stored on computer.

4. I use computers to find information for people. Readers come in with a lot of queries and I use either our own database or the national database that we're connected to to find what they want. They might want to know the name and address of a particular society, or last year's accounts of a company and we can find that out for them. Or they might want to find a particular newspaper article but they don't know the exact date it was published so we can find it for them by checking on our online database for anything they can remember: a name or the general topic. And we use computers to catalogue the books in the library and to record the books that readers borrow.

PHOTOCOPIABLE © Cambridge University Press 2002

---

entertainment software means more than just computer games. There are specialized programs for composing and playing music. PCs can combine sound, text and animated images. Multimedia applications allow users to produce slide shows, retouch photographs, etc. Optical disks make encyclopedias and books available on computer.

- *Factories:* Computers are used to control machinery, robots, production lines, lists of products, etc. By using computer-aided manufacturing software, engineers can simulate and test designs before parts are actually produced.
- *Hospitals:* Database programs are used to keep records of patients and medical personnel. Computers, monitors and scanners help doctors diagnose cancer and other illnesses. Electronic instruments and robots are used in surgery.

Completed grid for listening

Speaker	Job	What they use computers for
1	Composer	To record what he plays on keyboard To get different sounds from the synthesizers
2	Secretary	To write memos, letters, faxes To communicate with other offices by e-mail
3	Electrical engineer	To design electrical installations and lighting systems To make drawings To keep records (of tests)
4	Librarian	To find information for people To catalogue the books in the library To record the books that readers borrow

Unit 2 *Computer essentials*

Topic
The elements of a computer system

Learning objectives
To understand the basic structure of a computer system
To recognize differences between types of computers: mainframe, minicomputer, desktop PC, laptop and handheld computer
To use basic vocabulary connected with computers

Language
Grammar: Compound adjectives
Vocabulary: Basic terminology: *hardware, software, input, output, CPU, main memory, monitor, printer, keyboard, peripherals, storage devices, disk drives, mainframe, minicomputer, desktop, laptop, notebook, handheld*

Skills
Reading: Understanding specific information about the elements of a computer system
Matching slogans with components
Listening: Understanding the gist of a lecture about types of computer systems

Optional materials
A real computer system, computer magazines

Internet work
Wearable computers

Plan

Teacher's activities	Students' activities	Comments
1 Warm-up You can introduce the unit by asking SS 'What English words do you associate with "computer"?' Write the suggestions on the board. This will allow you to see the level and range of technical vocabulary they have. You may like to show them a real computer system and explain its components.	SS suggest words associated with 'computer' in a brainstorming exercise. In pairs SS label the elements of the computer system in the diagram. Then they read and check answers.	This unit may be a bit difficult for those who have never worked with a computer. Help them with technical aspects: **hardware** in contrast to **software**; **input** in contrast to **output** (see the diagram on page 8 of the Student's Book). We enter the data about the money received or paid out by a company during a given period (the **input**). Then, when a program is run, the computer processes the data. Finally, we can see the resulting balance (the **output**).
2 Reading Go round and check any problems with technical terms. You may wish to give SS a few tips about how to deal with vocabulary (see Introduction, page 2). Comprehension check: In whole-class feedback, ask for evidence from the text. This will help you assess SS' reading comprehension level.	SS use the information in the text and the diagram to do the matching exercise. They can confer in pairs. They can use their dictionaries or the Glossary, if necessary.	
3 Read and guess You may like to bring in some computer magazines and ask SS to find similar quotations.	SS decide individually. Whole-class checking.	

Unit 2 *Computer essentials*

4 **Get ready for listening** Encourage SS to talk about the computer they have at home, school or work. In preparation for the listening task you may like to pre-teach *mainframe, minicomputer, desktop computer, laptop, handheld.*	SS answer the questions orally.	
5 **Listening** A Check your answers with the whole class. B Tell SS to read the questions. Play the cassette, pausing after each paragraph (see Tapescript on page 10). Play the cassette again without pausing. Check answers with the whole class.	SS listen and label the pictures. Then they listen again and select the correct answer. SS compare answers in pairs.	SS should differentiate between different types of computer: mainframes, minicomputers, desktop PCs (kept on a desk) portables or laptops (sometimes held on one's lap), and handhelds or palmtops (held in one hand).
6 **Language work: Compound adjectives** Direct SS attention to the HELP box and set the task. Make sure they understand the text.	SS find the compound adjectives modifying the nouns and explain their meaning.	

Evaluation of the unit: ....
....

Answer key

1 Warm-up

Correctly labelled, the illustration should look like this:

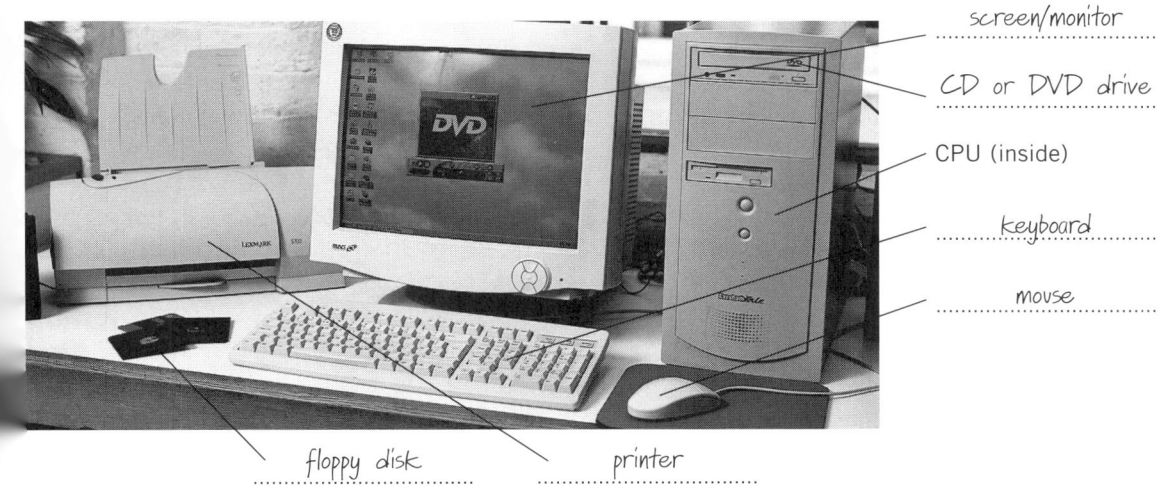

2 Reading

1 i 2 e 3 a 4 f 5 h
6 b 7 c 8 d 9 g

3 Read and guess

1 mouse   2 monitor   3 hard disk
4 CPU   5 printer

5 Listening

See tapescript in panel below.

A
a desktop PC
b minicomputer
c laptop
d mainframe
e handheld

B
1 b   2 b   3 a   4 b   5 a

6 Language work: Compound adjectives

battery-powered systems – systems that run on batteries

hands-free operation – operations that you make without using your hands

waist-mounted computer – computer worn on the user's waist

head-mounted display – a display which is worn on the user's head

voice-activated device – device which is worked by the user's voice

---

Tapescript

Digital computers can be divided into five main types, depending on their size and power: they are mainframes, minicomputers, desktop PCs, laptops and handheld computers.

'Mainframes' are the largest and most powerful computers. The basic configuration of a mainframe consists of a central system which processes immense amounts of data very quickly. This central system provides data information and computing facilities for hundreds of terminals connected together in a network. Mainframes are used by large companies, factories and universities.

'Minicomputers' are smaller and less powerful than mainframes. They can handle multi-tasking, that is, they can perform more than one task at the same time. Minicomputers are mainly used as file servers for terminals. Typical applications include academic computing, software engineering and other sophisticated applications in which many users share resources.

PCs carry out their processing on a single microchip. They are used as personal computers in the home or as workstations for a group. Typical examples are the IBM PC, or the Apple Macintosh. Broadly speaking, there are two classes of personal computer: (a) desktop PCs, which are designed to be placed on your desk, and (b) portable PCs, which can be used as a tiny notebook. This is why they are called 'notebooks' and 'laptops'. The latest models can run as fast as similar desktop computers and have similar configurations. They are ideal for business executives who travel a lot.

The smallest computers can be held in one hand. They're called handheld computers or palmtops. They are used as PC companions or as electronic organizers for storing notes, reminders and addresses.

PHOTOCOPIABLE © Cambridge University Press 2002

Unit 3 *Inside the system*

Topic
The central processing unit and the main memory

Learning objectives
To understand the structure of the central processing unit, and the functions of its different elements
To distinguish between main memory (RAM and ROM) and secondary storage

Language
Grammar: Contextual reference
Defining relative clauses
Vocabulary: *microprocessor, silicon chip, control unit, arithmetic logic unit, register, expansion slot, clock speed, main memory, gigahertz.*
Abbreviations and acronyms: *CPU, ALU, RAM, ROM, MHz, GHz, SIMM, DIMM*

Skills
Reading: Understanding the basic structure of the CPU
Understanding the different types of memory
Listening: Transferring information from a description to a diagram
Speaking: Describing one's ideal computer system

Optional materials
A real microprocessor chip; memory chips

Technical help is given on page 15

Internet work
Acronym finder

Plan

Teacher's activities	Students' activities	Comments
1 Warm-up This task introduces words which appear in the reading passage; some may be new to SS. Ask for answers in whole-class feedback.	SS translate technical specifications. They try to answer the questions.	Some SS may have problems with new terminology. Let them use the Glossary.
2 Reading **A** Encourage SS to work out the meaning of unfamiliar words for themselves; but make it clear also that they can ask questions if they need to. CPUs are the heart of computers. Ask SS to examine Figure 1 which illustrates the organization of a CPU. You may like to show them a real CPU chip.	**A** SS read the text and decide individually whether the statements are true or false. Then they confer in pairs and rewrite the false statements.	If you want to show SS the microprocessor and RAM chips, ask a computer science teacher to open a system unit so that SS can see the logic board of the computer.
B Explain that reference markers (personal pronouns, demonstrative pronouns, etc.) provide discourse cohesion and help us to understand the organization of ideas. Check answers with the whole class.	**B** SS find out what the words in bold refer to.	

11

3 Language work: Relative clauses A good opportunity to recycle the use of *who/that/which*. Check answers with the whole class.	SS work alone or in pairs.	Some SS may not understand the difference between defining and non-defining relative clauses. Provide some examples to show them. Check that SS understand when the relative can be omitted.
4 Listening This task revises the constituent parts of a computer system.	SS listen and label the diagram with the correct technical words.	
5 Vocabulary quiz Time the activity carefully. Give the answers and identify the winners.	SS do the quiz in groups of three. They write their answers.	
6 Your ideal computer system Circulate and listen to SS' descriptions.	SS make notes about their ideal computer and describe it to their partners.	

Evaluation of the unit: ....
....

Answer key

1 Warm-up

B
1 The main function of the microprocessor is to process the instructions provided by the software. It also coordinates the activities of the other units.
2 The megahertz (or the gigahertz). One MHz is equivalent to one million cycles per second. One GHz is equivalent to one thousand MHz.
3 'RAM' stands for 'random access memory'.

2 Reading

A
1 T   2 T   3 F   4 T
5 F   6 T   7 F   8 T

3 64-bit processors can handle more information than 32-bit processors.
5 RAM and ROM are types of internal memory. (Secondary storage is a type of memory which holds information permanently (e.g. disks). Perhaps the confusion is due to the fact that internal memory and secondary storage are both measured in megabytes.)

7 RAM (random access memory) is temporary, i.e. its information is lost when the computer is switched off.
(Permanent storage is provided by tapes, magnetic and optical disks.)

B Contextual reference

1 **which** refers to 'a single microprocessor chip – an integrated circuit –'
2 **that** refers to 'the instruction'
3 **they** refers to 'microprocessors'
4 **it** refers to 'an application'
5 **its** refers to the 'RAM'
6 **that** refers to 'expansion slots'

3 Language work: Relative clauses

1 That's the CPU **which/that** I'd like to buy. *or* That's the CPU I'd like to buy. (The relative pronoun can be omitted.)
2 A co-processor is an extra processor chip **which/that** does calculations at high speed.
3 The microprocessor coordinates the activities **which/that** take place in the computer system.
4 Last night I met someone **who/that** works for GM as a computer programmer.
5 A palmtop is a computer **which/that** is small enough to be held in the palm of the hand.
6 A megahertz is a unit of frequency **which/that** is used to measure processor speed.
7 Here's the DVD **which/that** you lent me! *or* Here's the DVD you lent me! (The relative pronoun can be omitted.)

4 Listening

See tapescript in panel below and completed chart on page 14.

Tapescript

A computer system consists of two parts: the software and the hardware. The software is the information in the form of data and program instructions. The hardware components are the electronic and mechanical parts of the system. The basic structure of a computer system is made up of three main hardware sections: (i) the central processing unit or CPU, (ii) the main memory, and (iii) the peripherals.

The CPU is a microprocessor chip which executes program instructions and coordinates the activities of all the other components. In order to improve the computer's performance, the user can add expansion cards for video, sound and networking.

The main memory holds the instructions and data which are currently being processed by the CPU.

The internal memory of a microcomputer is usually composed of two sections: RAM (random access memory) and ROM (read only memory).

The peripherals are the physical units attached to the computer. They include input/output devices as well as storage devices. Input devices enable us to present information to the computer; for example, the keyboard and the mouse. Output devices allow us to extract the results from the computer; for example, we can see the output on the monitor or in printed form. Secondary storage devices such as floppy, hard and optical disks are used to store information permanently. For example, we use CDs and DVDs to store large amounts of information.

PHOTOCOPIABLE © Cambridge University Press 2002

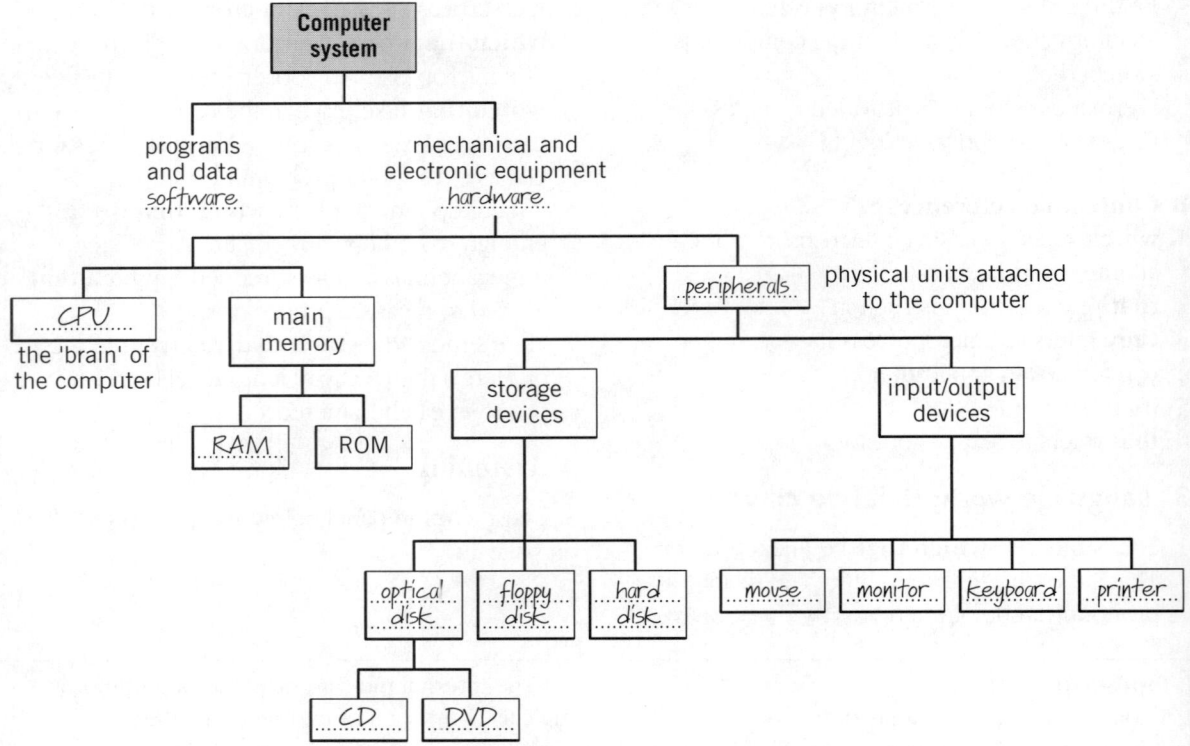

5 Vocabulary quiz

1. The control unit (CU), the arithmetic logic unit (ALU) and the registers
2. Random access memory
3. ROM
4. The information contained in the RAM section
5. Megabyte, Mega or MB
6. Single In-line Memory Module
7. A megahertz is equivalent to one million cycles per second. It is the unit used to measure the processor speed.
8. The arithmetic logic unit. It performs mathematical calculations and logical operations.
9. Bit
10. We use magnetic disks (floppies or hard disks), optical disks, etc.

Technical help
The CPU, the heart of the computer

The CPU, or central processing unit, is just a tiny microprocessor chip, about the size of a postage stamp, but it holds more than forty million transistors and functions as the nerve centre of the entire computer.

The CPU is the part of the computer that processes data and instructions. Its key components are: a control unit, arithmetic logic unit, a clock and some memory registers.

The two main manufacturers of microprocessor chips are Intel and Motorola.

1. The Intel 80x86 chips were used in the first IBM PCs and compatibles. In 1993, Intel Corp. introduced the Pentium processor, which was 150 times faster than the speediest 8086. Now most PCs have Intel Pentium 4 or AMD chips, delivering high performance for multimedia, Internet communications and 3-D applications (see below).

2. The Motorola 680x0 chips were used in the first Macintosh, Atari ST and Amiga computers. In 1993, the alliance of IBM, Apple and Motorola created the PowerPC, a new 64-bit processor that could handle more information than 32-bit processors. Today, Macs have a PowerPC G3 or G4 processor, with high-performance multimedia extensions and faster clock speeds (see below).

Intel chips

MIPS*: 0.33 at launch
0.75 highest
Transistors: 29,000

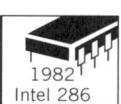
MIPS: 1.2 at launch
2.6 highest
Transistors: 130,000

MIPS: 5 at launch
11 highest
Transistors: 275,000

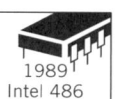
MIPS: 20 at launch
54 highest
Transistors: 1.2 million

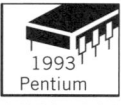
MIPS: 112
Transistors: 3.1 million

Transistors: 7.5 million

Transistors: 9.5 million

Transistors: 42 million

Motorola chips

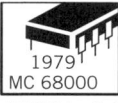
MIPS*: 0.5
Transistors: 70,000

MIPS: 5
Transistors: 300,000

MIPS: 15
Transistors: 1.2 million

Power PC
developed by IBM, Apple and Motorola

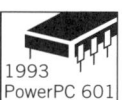
Transistors: 2.8 million

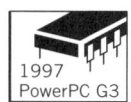
Transistors: 6.5 million

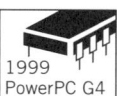
The next generation may reach 50 million transistors.

*MIPS=millions of instructions per second

Unit 4 *Bits and bytes*

Topics
Units of memory. Binary notation

Learning objectives
To understand the value of different units of memory (bits, bytes, KB, MB, GB)
To build up new words by using prefixes
To understand the relation between pixels (on the screen) and bits (in memory)

Language
Vocabulary: Units of memory (*bits, bytes, KB, MB, GB*); *ASCII code, binary notation, decimal notation, bit-mapped display*

Prefixes: *deci-, kilo-, mega-, giga-, mini-, micro-, mono-, multi-, bi-*, etc.

Skills
Reading: Understanding the units of memory in a computer
Understanding how bits are used to create the display on the screen
Writing: Translating

Optional materials
ASCII code chart

Technical help is given on pages 18 and 19

Internet work
Online computer dictionaries

Plan

Teacher's activities	Students' activities	Comments
1 Reading You may want to introduce the theme by writing the words *bits* and *bytes* on the board and asking SS to explain the difference between these terms. Check answers with the whole class. Make sure SS understand the function of the ASCII code. Give them the ASCII code chart if the need arises. **2 Word building** Explain that these prefixes are frequently used in technical English. Check answers to **B** with the whole class if done in class (this could be set for homework). **3 Bits for pictures** Check SS understand the relation between pixels (on the screen) and bits (in memory). Explain the difference between the primary colours – red, green and blue – in computers, and the basic colours used as pigments: magenta, yellow and cyan.	With the help of a partner, SS should try to answer the questions before they read. SS read the passage and check their predictions. SS write a sentence explaining the meaning of some expressions. **B** SS read and match the terms with the appropriate explanations. **C** SS translate the last paragraph of the text. SS explain the calculations made to obtain a palette of 16.7 million colours.	Some SS may have problems with the concepts underlying this topic. Just make sure they understand the basic terminology: *bit, byte, kilobyte, megabyte,* etc. One important aspect of data storage is the format in which it is stored. Most computers can save and retrieve TEXT or ASCII files. This format allows different computers to exchange text files. ASCII codes are conventionally expressed in the decimal system, but hexadecimal and octal notations are also frequent (see Technical help on pages 18 and 19).

> Evaluation of the unit: ....
> ....

Answer key

1 Reading

A

1. A binary system uses two digits (0 and 1). Switches inside a computer can only be in one of two possible states: OFF or ON. To represent these two conditions we use binary notation: 0 means OFF and 1 means ON. Each 0 or 1 is called a **bi**nary digi**t**, or **bit**.
2. In binary notation, numbers are represented by two digits: 0 and 1. In the decimal system we use ten digits. For example: the binary number 10 represents 2 in the decimal system.
3. A byte
4. 1 megabyte = one million bytes (or 1,024 kilobytes)
   1 gigabyte = one thousand million bytes (or 1,024 megabytes)
5. 'ASCII' stands for 'American Standard Code for Information Interchange'. The purpose of this code is to provide a standard system for the representation of characters.

C

1 byte   2 kilobyte   3 megabyte   4 gigabyte

2 Word building

B

1. A minicomputer is smaller and less powerful than a mainframe, but is usually bigger than a microcomputer.
2. The term 'microcomputer' is used to define small desktop computers.
3. The decimal system is the system in which the ten digits 0 to 9 are used.
4. The hexadecimal system is the notation of numbers to the base or radix of sixteen.
5. A multi-user configuration is a system in which many users are connected to the central computer.
6. A bidimensional chessboard is displayed or drawn in two dimensions.
7. A tricycle is a three-wheeled cycle.
8. A monochrome computer has a monitor which displays one colour at a time.
9. A CPU with 256 megabytes of RAM is a computer with 256,000,000 bytes of RAM.
10. A document of 3 KB occupies 3,000 bytes.

3 Bits for pictures

B

1 e   2 d   3 a   4 c   5 b

C

Calculations
- Bits can be either 1 or 0 (2 positions)
- There are 3 primary colours
- We have 8 bits per colour

This gives a palette of $(2^3)^8 = 16.7$ million colours.

Technical help

Binary code

A computer can only manipulate 1s and 0s in order to process information. A 1 is represented by current flowing through a wire and a 0 by no current flowing through the wire. Sometimes 1 is referred to as a high voltage and 0 is referred as a low voltage. Everything about computers is based upon this binary process.

Each digit – 1 or 0 – is called a **bit**. Eight bits together are called a **byte**. The ASCII code is just a standard system to represent characters as bytes of binary signals.

ASCII, which stands for 'American Standard Code for Information Interchange', permits

ASCII code chart

b7	0	0	0	0	1	1	1	1
b6	0	0	1	1	0	0	1	1
b5	0	1	0	1	0	1	0	1
BITS b4 b3 b2 b1	Control special characters		Symbols Numbers		UPPER CASE characters		Lower case characters	
0 0 0 0	NUL 0	DLE 16	SP 32	0 48	@ 64	P 80	` 96	p 112
0 0 0 1	SOH 1	DC1 17	! 33	1 49	A 65	Q 81	a 97	q 113
0 0 1 0	STX 2	DC2 18	" 34	2 50	B 66	R 82	b 98	r 114
0 0 1 1	ETX 3	DC3 19	# 35	3 51	C 67	S 83	c 99	s 115
0 1 0 0	EOT 4	DC4 20	$ 36	4 52	D 68	T 84	d 100	t 116
0 1 0 1	ENQ 5	NAK 21	% 37	5 53	E 69	U 85	e 101	u 117
0 1 1 0	ACK 6	SYN 22	& 38	6 54	F 70	V 86	f 102	v 118
0 1 1 1	BEL 7	ETB 23	' 39	7 55	G 71	W 87	g 103	w 119
1 0 0 0	BS 8	CAN 24	(40	8 56	H 72	X 88	h 104	x 120
1 0 0 1	HT 9	EM 25	) 41	9 57	I 73	Y 89	i 105	y 121
1 0 1 0	LF 10	SUB 26	* 42	: 58	J 74	Z 90	j 106	z 122
1 0 1 1	VT 11	ESC 27	+ 43	; 59	K 75	[91	k 107	{ 123
1 1 0 0	FF 12	FS 28	, 44	< 60	L 76	\ 92	l 108	| 124
1 1 0 1	CR 13	GS 29	- 45	= 61	M 77	] 93	m 109	} 125
1 1 1 0	SO 14	RS 30	. 46	> 62	N 78	^ 94	n 110	~ 126
1 1 1 1	SI 15	US 31	/ 47	? 63	O 79	_ 95	o 111	DEL 127

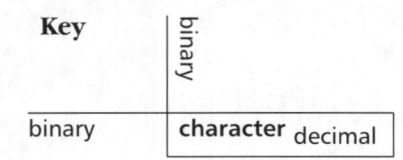

Key

binary	
binary	character decimal

PHOTOCOPIABLE © Cambridge University Press 2002

computers from different manufacturers to exchange data. ASCII uses 7-digit binary numbers to represent the letters of the alphabet, the numbers 0 to 9, various punctuation marks and symbols, and some special functions such as the carriage return. Seven digits in binary implies that ASCII has room for 128 characters or symbols (with seven places to arrange 1s and 0s, we can make 128 possible code combinations). The eighth, or left-most bit of each byte, is often used to make sure the other seven bits are sent and received correctly (see the illustration below). Some programs use this bit for specific purposes.

When you press a key on the computer keyboard, your program translates that key press into an ASCII code. This code can represent a character, or a function to be performed.

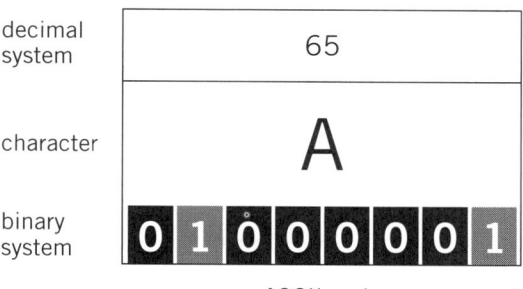

ASCII code

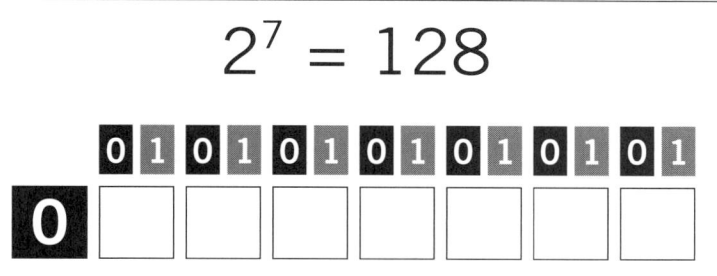

Notations

ASCII codes are conventionally expressed in decimal notation because decimal numbers are more convenient for people to recognize and interpret than binary numbers (see the ASCII code chart on page 18).

In programming it is also common to represent binary codes by means of hexadecimal or octal notations. In hexadecimal notation, 16 is the base or radix. The ten digits 0 to 9 are used, and in addition six more digits, usually A, B, C, D, E and F, to represent 10, 11, 12, 13, 14 and 15 as single characters. Octal notation uses eight digits: 0, 1, 2, 3, 4, 5, 6, 7.

These notations are used to write software, as a shorthand way of representing long strings of bits. Thus the string 01000001 can be represented as octal 101, decimal 65 and hexadecimal 41.

Binary	Octal	Decimal	Hexadecimal
0000000	000	000	00
0000001	001	001	01
0000010	002	002	02
0000011	003	003	03
0000100	004	004	04
0000101	005	005	05
0000110	006	006	06
0000111	007	007	07
0001000	**010**	008	08
0001001	011	009	09
0001010	012	**010**	0A
0001011	013	011	0B
0001100	014	012	0C
0001101	015	013	0D
0001110	016	014	0E
0001111	017	015	0F
0010000	020	016	**10**

Octal and hexadecimal notations arose from the need to handle data in 8-bit and 16-bit microprocessors

Unit 5 *Buying a computer*

Topic
In a computer shop. Computers for particular work situations

Learning objectives
To enquire about computers in a shop
To understand technical specifications of different computers
To select the most suitable computers for particular people

Language
Language of enquiry

Revision of terminology, displayed on a vocabulary tree

Skills
Listening: Listening for specific information and language in a dialogue
Speaking: Role play in a computer shop
Reading: Understanding technical specifications
Writing: Writing a letter to a friend, recommending a computer

Plan

Teacher's activities	Students' activities	Comments
1 Before you listen Check suggestions with the whole class. Write them on the board and practise their pronunciation as necessary.	SS work individually as they list the items.	
2 Listening A Play the cassette and check answers with the whole class. If necessary, play the cassette again. B Help SS distinguish between real information and those expressions used to maintain conversation (*er, um, well, you see, I mean*). Check answers with the whole class.	A SS listen and fill in the missing information. They first work individually, then check answers with a partner. B SS listen to part of the dialogue and fill in the gaps.	
3 Role play Give SS time to read the information and instructions. Then go round and check pronunciations, lexis and structures. **Option:** Leave the task 'open', without guided steps, so that SS can be as creative as they want.	In pairs, SS do the role play, following the instructions.	This task, together with the previous one, will help SS to acquire the language needed for purchasing a computer. SS may not be used to this sort of guided role play.

4 Read and talk Check answers to **A** and **B** with the whole class and ask them to justify their choices. **5 Vocabulary tree** You can ask a S to draw the tree on the board. Check answers with the whole class. Encourage SS to construct similar trees or networks for other word fields. **6 Writing** You could set this for homework.	**A** SS read the descriptions and in pairs choose a computer for each person. **B** SS choose the computer closest to their ideal system they described in Unit 3. SS insert the words in the appropriate place on the vocabulary tree. SS write a letter recommending a computer to a friend.	This task, together with Tasks 5 and 6, allows you to check that SS have understood the concepts and information introduced in the previous units.

Evaluation of the unit: ....
....

Answer key

1 Before you listen

Possible answers

A computer, a hard disk, a Zip drive, a tape drive, CD-ROMs, a DVD drive, diskettes, RAM chips, a colour monitor, a scanner, a digital camera, a plotter, a printer, a mouse, a modem, accessories (a security kit, an anti-glare filter, etc.), all kinds of software products.

2 Listening

See tapescript in panel on page 22.

A
iMac
Processor speed **1 GHz**
RAM standard **256 MB**
Hard disk capacity **40 GB**
Price **£1,425**
DVD and MAC OS included? **Yes**

iBook
Processor speed **700 MHz**
RAM standard **128 MB**
Hard disk capacity **20 GB**
Price **£1,207**
DVD and MAC OS included? **Yes**

B
1 models
2 microprocessor
3 running
4 faster
5 RAM
6 expanded
7 640 MB

4 Read and talk

Daniel: the Compaq Presario PC
Sarah: the Power Mac G4
Andy: the Sun workstation
Tanya: the Compaq notebook

Tapescript

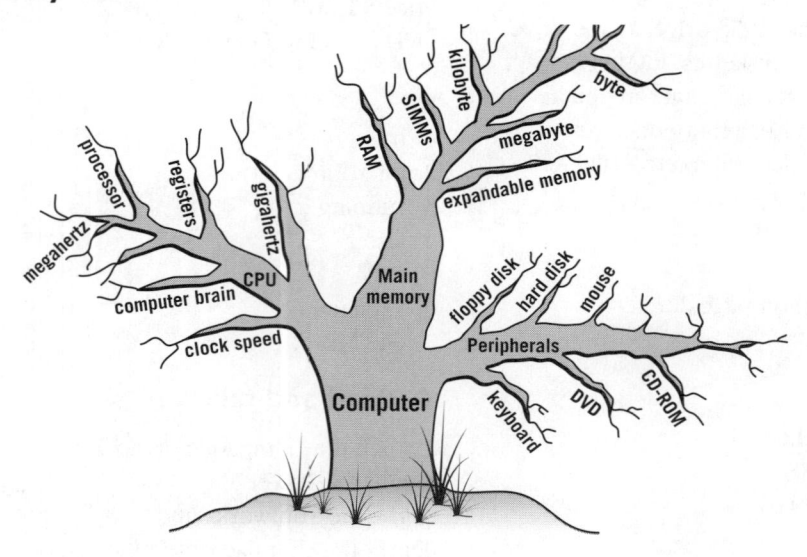

Input/output devices

Unit		page
6	*Type, click and talk!*	24
7	*Capture your favourite image*	27
8	*Viewing the output*	31
9	*Choosing a printer*	35
10	*I/O devices for the disabled*	39

Unit 6 *Type, click and talk!*

Topic
Input devices: the keyboard and the mouse
Voice input

Learning objectives
To be able to describe input devices
To identify different keys on a keyboard and explain their function
To understand basic mouse actions

Language
Grammar: Describing objects: *for* + *ing;* relative pronoun + verb; relative pronoun + *is used* + *to* + infinitive; *used* + *to* + infinitive
Vocabulary: *keyboard, mouse, scanner, trackball, graphics tablet, lightpen, joystick, voice recognition device.* Symbols and groups of keys. Mouse actions: *select, click, double-click, drag*

Skills
Listening: Identifying particular devices from descriptions
Understanding features of speech recognition technology
Writing: Describing a joystick
Speaking: Exchanging information about different types of input devices
Reading: Identifying keys on a diagram from information in the text
Reading for specific information

Optional materials
Real objects from the computer classroom
A standard keyboard

Internet work
Talk to your computer

Plan

Teacher's activities	Students' activities	Comments
Section page You may want to point out the learning objectives to your SS.	SS familiarize themselves with the topics and objectives of the section.	
1 Interacting with your computer Introduce the theme by directing SS' attention to the pictures. Then ask SS to read the introductory definition. Explain *input* in contrast to *output*.	SS look at the illustrations and try to name the devices.	
2 Listening Stop the cassette after each description.	SS listen and identify the three input devices.	
3 Language work Write the syntactic patterns on the board. Check that they understand the use of *to* + infinitive.	SS describe the joystick in a short paragraph, using different constructions. First they work alone, then confer in pairs.	This task is designed to help SS describe computer devices. Some students will produce wrong sentences like **for to control*.
4 Speaking Check that they use suitable structures for describing objects.	SS work in pairs. One person describes a device; the other person guesses what it is. They should not look at each other's notes.	

5 About the keyboard

A If possible, show SS a real keyboard. Ask them to check if the illustration in their books is an exact reproduction of the real thing.

B Encourage SS to learn new terminology.

SS can justify their answers in their mother tongue. They may want to talk about the purpose of 'special' keys.

6 Mouse actions

Make sure SS understand the basic mouse techniques: *select, click, double-click, drag, grab*.

SS read the text and fill in the gaps with verbs from the list.

7 Listening

A Ask SS if they have ever used their voice to input data. Go through the list of features before playing the audio material.

B Provide more examples illustrating the meaning of these modal verbs, if necessary.

A SS listen and tick (✓) the features mentioned in the interview.

B SS revise the use of some modal verbs.

Some SS may have problems with the task. Give them a copy of the tapescript.

Evaluation of the unit: ....
....

Answer key

1 Interacting with your computer

1 lightpen
2 joystick
3 scanner
4 mouse
5 keyboard
6 graphics tablet
7 trackball
8 voice recognition device

2 Listening

See tapescript in panel.
1 keyboard   2 mouse   3 lightpen

3 Language work

Possible answers

- A joystick is an input device which is used to play games. The user takes hold of a lever to control and move the cursor around the screen.
- A joystick is a device for controlling and moving the cursor around the screen in computer games.
- A joystick is a device with a vertical lever which is used to control the cursor in computer games.

Tapescript

1 This device is used to enter information into the computer. As well as having normal typewriter keys for characters and a numeric keypad, it may also have function keys and editing keys for special purposes.

2 This is a device for controlling the cursor and selecting items on the screen. The ball underneath is rolled in any direction across the surface of a table to move the cursor on the screen. By clicking a button, the user can activate icons or select items and text.

3 In shape, this input device is similar to an ordinary pen. It works by detecting light from the computer screen and is used by pointing directly at the screen display. It allows the user to answer multiple-choice questions and to draw diagrams or graphics.

PHOTOCOPIABLE © Cambridge University Press 2002

4 Speaking

Student A	Student B
1 scanner	1 trackball
2 voice recognition device	2 graphics tablet

5 About the keyboard

A

1 Alphanumeric keys. (Note: The layout of alphanumeric keys is known as QWERTY because the first six letters at the top left of the keyboard are the letters Q, W, E, R, T and Y.)
2 Function keys: these are labelled F1–F12
3 Numeric keypad: this is on the right
4 Editing keys: these are the arrow keys (↑, ↓, ←, →), Pg Up, Pg Down, Home, End, Ins, Del
5 Special keys: Ctrl, Alt, Alt Gr, Esc, Enter (Return), Tab, Caps Lock, Shift, Print Screen, Scroll Lock

B

1 Space bar
2 Return
3 Escape
4 Alt
5 Backspace
6 Shift
7 Caps lock
8 Tab
9 Arrow keys

6 Mouse actions

1 control 2 move 3 click 4 select
5 drag 6 grab 7 double-click

7 Listening

See tapescript in panel.

A
- ✓ have a good sound card and a microphone
- ✓ take dictation with accuracy
- — create and compile a computer program
- ✓ surf the Web by speaking
- ✓ execute programs and navigate around menus by voice commands
- — design graphics

B

1 should 2 can 3 must 4 could
5 will

Tapescript

Interviewer: Mobile phones and the Internet have changed the way we communicate. However, we still need to use the keyboard and the mouse to communicate with computers. When shall we be able to interact with PCs by voice?

Anne: Well, the technology already exists but the habit of talking to a computer is only just beginning to take off.

Interviewer: What are the basic components of a speech-recognition system?

Anne: Basically you need voice-recognition software, a sound card and a microphone. If you want to have good results, you should get a high-quality headset microphone.

Interviewer: Right. What sort of things can you do with a speech-recognition system?

Anne: The system converts voice into text, so you can dictate text directly onto your word processor or e-mail program. The technology is particularly useful to dictate notes, business memos, letters and e-mail.

Interviewer: But is dictation accurate, I mean, does the system interpret all the words correctly?

Anne: Speech companies claim an accuracy rate of around 98 per cent. But the system is more accurate if you train the software by reading aloud sample text for a few minutes. This process teaches the program to recognize words that are not in its built-in dictionary, for example, proper names, abbreviations, unusual words, etc.

Interviewer: OK. And can you execute programs and navigate around menus and windows?

Anne: Yes, you can control your PC by voice commands. This means you can launch programs, open a file, save it in a particular format or print it. Some systems even let you search the Web by voice or chat using your voice instead of the keyboard.

Interviewer: That sounds exciting. And how do you see the future of speech-recognition?

Anne: In a few years' time, I think a lot of people will use their voices to interact with computers. Some day, we'll be talking to our PC naturally, like a friend.

PHOTOCOPIABLE © Cambridge University Press 2002

Unit 7 *Capture your favourite image*

Topic	Vocabulary: *scan, flatbed scanner, slide scanner,*

Topic
Scanners

Learning objectives
To show understanding of written texts about a scanner, a digital camera and a camcorder
To distinguish between facts and opinions in advertisements
To distinguish between different types of scanners

Language
  Grammar: Comparatives and superlatives of adjectives

Vocabulary: *scan, flatbed scanner, slide scanner, handheld scanner, digitized image, digital camera, camcorder (video camera)*. Suffixes to form adjectives and nouns. Persuasive words in advertisements

Skills
  Listening: Completing notes
  Reading: Finding specific information. Distinguishing facts and opinions in advertisements

Optional materials
  Advertisements from specialist magazines

Plan

Teacher's activities	*Students' activities*	*Comments*
1 The eyes of your computer You can introduce the theme by asking questions like: 'What does the title of the lesson suggest to you?', 'Why are scanners and cameras called the "eyes" of your computer?' Direct SS' attention to the illustrations. Check answers with the whole class.	Using the information in the texts and the illustrations, SS answer the questions.	You may like to explain the word *scanner*. The verb *scan* has two different meanings: – When you *scan* written material, you look through it in order to find important information. – If a machine *scans* something, it reads or examines it very quickly, by moving a beam of light or electrons over it.
2 Listening Ask SS to read the notes before listening. Check their answers in whole-class feedback.	SS listen to the conversation and complete the notes.	
3 Facts and opinions Make clear the differences between facts and opinions. Write the chart on the board and complete it with SS' answers.	In small groups, SS read the advertisements and fill in the chart. SS discuss their answers.	This task aims to point out the difference between facts and opinions and to highlight the persuasive language used in advertisements.

4 Language work: Comparatives and superlatives Let SS explain the rules in their mother tongue.	SS deduce the grammatical rules for forming comparative and superlative adjectives.	More work on this grammatical area is in Unit 9.
5 Word building Explain these two types of suffixes. Remind SS of the importance of word formation processes.	SS put the words in the box into the two columns.	
6 Advertisement: A digital camera This authentic advert illustrates some of the persuasive language of advertising.	Alone or in pairs. SS choose words from the box and complete the advert.	

Evaluation of the unit: ....
....

Answer key

1 The eyes of your computer

1 A scanner.
2 A colour scanner operates by using three rotating lamps which have red, green and blue filters. The software combines the separate images into a single colour.
3 Digital cameras don't use film. Photos are stored in the camera's memory chip as digital data (binary codes made up of 1s and 0s).
4 A camcorder, or digital video camera.
5 Video editing software.
6 Scanners can be a real help in reading information from forms, manuscripts and other documents and converting them into data that can then be edited. They are also useful for producing images for reports, leaflets, presentations, etc.
Digital cameras can be plugged into a computer to download and edit photos using a program like Adobe Photoshop. Home users may like to use digital video cameras to make home movies. In business DV cameras can be used for teleconferencing, where several people are connected on a network. This allows participants to see images of each other, accompanied by text and voice.

2 Listening

See tapescript in panel on page 29.
1 The technology used in scanners is similar to that used in **photocopiers**.
2 A laser beam reads the image in **horizontal lines**.
3 The image is then **sent to the computer**.
4 Text is scanned with **OCR software**.
5 Flatbed scanners can scan **text, colour pictures and even small three-dimensional objects**.
6 Slide scanners are used to scan **35 mm slides or film negatives**.
7 Handheld scanners are used for capturing **small pictures or logos**.

Tapescript

Student: What sort of technology is used in scanners?

Vicky: Well, a scanner is a bit like a photocopier. You put the image you want to copy face down on the glass plate of the scanner, start the program, and a laser beam reads the image in horizontal lines. This image is then sent to the computer where you can see it, changing it as you want.

Student: What about text? Can you scan text?

Vicky: Yes, you can, but you need special software called OCR – optical character recognition. This interprets the text letter-by-letter and enables the computer to recognize the characters.

Student: Why do people need to scan text?

Vicky: Well, text that's been scanned can be stored as data in databases, or edited with a word processor.

Student: Eh, what types of scanners are there?

Vicky: Well, there are three basic types: flatbed scanners, slide scanners and handheld scanners. Flatbed scanners are built like a photocopier and are for use on a desktop. They can scan text, colour pictures and even small three-dimensional objects. They are very convenient and versatile. Slide scanners are used to scan 35 mm slides or film negatives. They work at very high resolution, so they are more expensive than flatbeds. Handheld scanners are small, compact and T-shaped. The scanning head is not as wide as the one in a flatbed – they can only copy images up to about 4 inches wide. They are used for capturing small pictures and logos. They are very cheap, but their appeal has diminished because they are not very useful for OCR, scanning in colour images can be a laborious process, and the quality ...

PHOTOCOPIABLE © Cambridge University Press 2002

3 Facts and opinions

A

	ColourScan XR	*ScanPress 800*
Facts	Flatbed scanner 600 dpi of resolution 9" × 15" of scanning area You can enter data and graphic images directly into word processors or databases. Comes with its own image-capture software which allows for colour and grey retouching. £290	Self-calibrating, flatbed scanner 800 dpi of resolution You can scan black-and-white and colour images. Includes JPEG technology to compress and decompress images. Comes with OCR software and Adobe Photoshop. £510
Opinions	You can get crisp, clean scans ... ... it's easy to use. It couldn't be cheaper. ... a clear winner.	... the highest technology ... the best scans with the least effort. ... images with high colour definition and sharpness. This is a fantastic machine you will love working with. ... only £510 ... ... an excellent investment.

B
Possible answers
1. The one for ScanPress 800.
2. Both texts give a similar amount of objective information.

4 Language work: Comparatives and superlatives

1. and 2 *faster* and *cheaper:* The comparative of one-syllable adjectives is formed by adding *-er*.
2. *the highest:* The superlative of one-syllable adjectives is formed with the suffix *-est*.
3. *the cleverest:* Two-syllable adjectives usually form the superlative with *-est*. (In some cases it is also formed with *most*.)
4. *the most revolutionary:* Adjectives with three or more syllables form the superlative with *most*.
5. *the best* and *the least:* Irregular superlative forms of *good* and *little*.
6. *more accurate:* Adjectives with three or more syllables form the comparative with *more*.
7. *more easily* and *look better:* The comparatives of adverbs are formed in a similar way to those of adjectives. *Better* is the comparative of *well*.

5 Word building

Adjectives	Nouns
self-calibrating	computer
easy	resolution
printed	sharpness
personal	information
capable	compression
useful	technology
expensive	calculator
reducible	assistant
	possibility
	investment

6 Advertisement: A digital camera

1. easy-to-use
2. fashionable
3. wide
4. vivid
5. shots
6. faster

Unit 8   *Viewing the output*

Topics
CRT monitors and flat screens
Health and safety with computers

Learning objectives
To understand how a computer display works
To explain tables or charts with technical specifications about monitors
To understand warnings and instructions for the use of the monitor

Language
Grammar: Instructions and advice: imperatives, *should, ought to*
Vocabulary: *pixel, resolution, hertz, flicker, phosphor, electron beam, refresh rate, bit-mapped display, ergonomics, tilt-and-swivel,*
extremely low frequency emissions
Abbreviations: *VDU, CRT, LCD, dpi*

Skills
Speaking: Describing the screen of a computer
Reading: Understanding technical explanations
Writing: Writing a description from information in a table
Listening: Listening for specific information in order to complete sentences

Optional materials
The reference manual of a monitor
Screen standards and regulations

Internet work
Flat screens

Plan

Teacher's activities	*Students' activities*	*Comments*
1 Warm-up Encourage SS to think about the monitor they have at home or at school. You can ask individual SS to answer the questions. Point out that *colour* is British E., whereas *color* is American E. Give some other examples.	SS read the introduction. Then they think about a monitor and try to answer the questions.	*Monochrome* does not exactly mean 'black and white', but 'one colour' (black with a scale of grey shades). The size of a monitor is measured diagonally across the screen (e.g. 15, 17 inches).
2 Reading Direct SS' attention to the illustrations. Remind SS to use the context to guess unfamiliar words. It is possible to do the task without understanding every word.	SS try to deduce the meaning of unknown words and answer the questions. They compare their answers in pairs.	This is a technical theme which some SS may find difficult. Help them with new words.
3 Writing Point out how the description of Monitor A relates to the table. This will help them describe Monitor B.	SS read the technical specifications. Then they expand the details into descriptive sentences.	
4 Listening To introduce the topic, ask SS to look at the picture. Try to personalize the task. Ask questions like 'Do you use computers a lot?', 'Have you got a protective filter over the front of your monitor?'	SS look at the illustration and talk about their own experience. Then they listen and complete the captions.	*Ergonomics* is the study of fitting equipment to people so that it is easier to use and does not cause harm to users.

If there is a computer classroom at your school, ask SS some questions about the position of the monitors, distance between PCs, etc.	Then they write the number of each caption into the correct place in the picture.	If SS find the task difficult, give them copies of the tapescript.
5 Language work: Instructions and advice This revises the grammatical forms used to give instructions and advice. The task is directly related to the listening passage. Check that students know that this is the imperative. Point out that the infinitive is used after *should* and *ought to*. Check answers with the whole class	SS first work alone.	
Optional follow-up Ask SS to write down twelve words from the unit that they might use when talking about monitors. Ask them to choose three that are new to them and use them in three sentences.		

Evaluation of the unit: ....
....

Answer key

2 Reading

B

1 Pixel resolution – or density – affects the quality of the image. The same screen with more pixels produces a better picture.
2 The hertz, or Hz
3 Because a low refresh rate produces a flickering, unsteady screen.
4 Phosphor
5 VGA (video graphics array). (A standard developed by IBM.)
6 'LCD' stands for 'liquid-crystal display'. This kind of display is used in portable computers.

3 Writing

B

The details of Monitor B could be expanded into descriptive sentences like this:

1 This is a conventional Cathode Ray Tube monitor.
2 The size of the screen is 19 inches. (Note: 19-inch to 21-inch displays are appropriate for those applications that require detail, like electrical or mechanical CAD, 3-D modelling and industrial design. Similarly, magazine publishers require large monitors because they need to see two facing pages simultaneously.)
3 This display system has a resolution of 1,280 × 1,024 pixels. (Note: This is enough for WYSIWYG: 'what you see is what you get'.)
4 It can deliver 16.7 million colours.
5 The scan rate is 85 hertz, which means that this monitor will produce a steady, flicker-free picture.
6 The words 'tilt-and-swivel' mean that you can change the orientation of the monitor, i.e. you can move the monitor up, down and around.
7 It includes an anti-glare filter.

4 Listening

See tapescript in panel on page 33.

Tapescript

Tony: As you may know, researchers have begun to worry about the health risks of spending a lot of time in front of a computer. Anyone spending more than four hours a day working on a PC may start to suffer from aching hands, neck or shoulders, occasional headaches and eye strain. These can all make you feel irritable and stressed. Yes?

Student 1: Is there anything we can do to avoid these risks?

Tony: Yes, there's quite a lot you can do. For example, if you take the trouble to position your computer properly you can avoid backache. Get a good chair – one that supports your lower back and is adjustable so you can have both your feet on the floor. Position the keyboard at the same height as your elbows, with your arms parallel to the work surface, and position the monitor so it is at, or just below eye level. You should look down at it slightly, not up. Don't put your monitor in front of a window, and make sure that there isn't a lamp shining directly into your eyes or reflecting off the screen. The monitor should also be fitted with a tilt-and-swivel stand. Does anyone know what that is?

Student 2: Yes, I think it's a kind of stand that lets you move the monitor up or around so you can use it at the right angle and height.

Tony: Yes, that's right. Have any of you had any health problems from using a computer?

Student 3: Well, often my eyes feel really sore and tired after I've been using the computer for a few hours. How do I stop that happening?

Tony: Well, as a general rule, don't use a monitor that's fuzzy or that distorts the image. Give your eyes a rest – look away from the monitor from time to time, out of the window or across the room.

Student 4: I've heard that monitors can be dangerous because they emit electromagnetic radiation. Is that true?

Tony: Well, all monitors, except LCD displays, emit extremely low frequency radiation. We don't really know how serious prolonged exposure to this radiation can be but recent results are not very hopeful. To minimize your risk, stay at arm's length away from the front of the monitor when you're working. If you work in a room with a lot of computers, make sure you sit at least 1 m 20 cm away from the sides or backs of any monitors as the radiation fields can be strong there.

Student 5: What do you think of radiation guards? Are they really useful?

Tony: Yes, I think they are. As you know, they're protective filters that fit over the front of the monitor. They can't absorb all the ELF radiation but they do reduce it substantially. Anyway, the effects of radiation from screens are still being studied, so don't get too alarmed.

(Adapted from *Understanding Computers*, N. Shedroff *et al.*, Sybex, 1992, pp. 39–41)

PHOTOCOPIABLE © Cambridge University Press 2002

1. You should get a good chair, one that **supports your lower back and is adjustable so that you can have both feet on the floor**.
2. Position the keyboard **at the same height as your elbows, with your arms parallel to the work surface**.
3. Position the monitor **at eye level, or just below**.
4. A tilt-and-swivel display lets you **move the monitor up or around, so you can use it at the right angle and height**.
5. You should stay an arm's length away from **the front of the monitor**.
6. If you work in a room with a lot of computers, sit **at least 1 m 20 cm away from the sides or backs of the other monitors**.

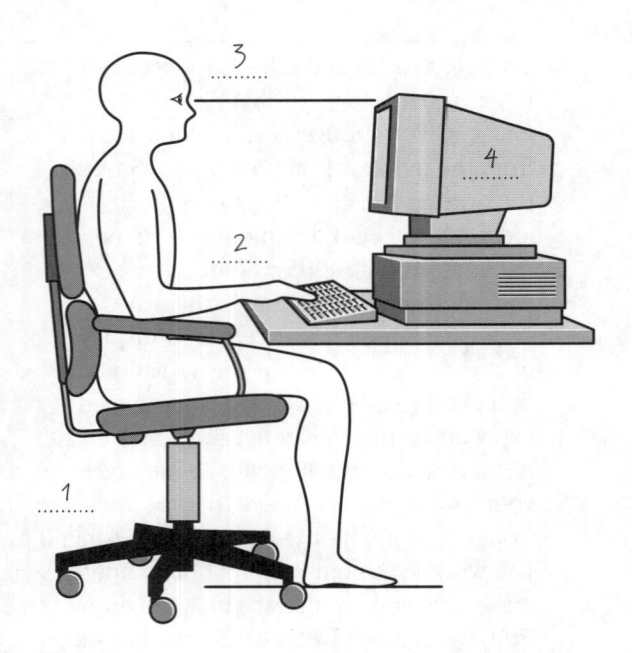

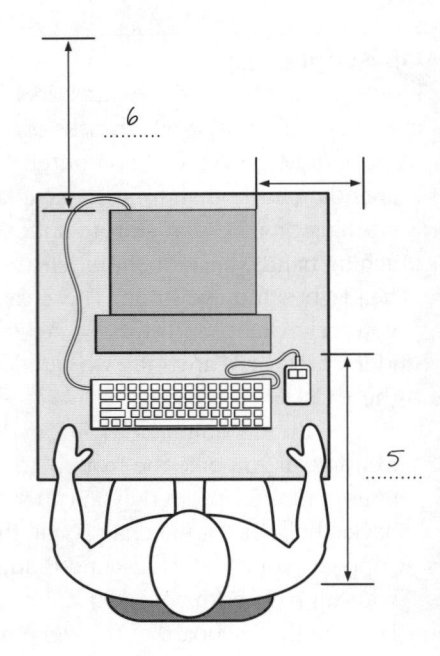

5 Language work: Instructions and advice

1 You shouldn't/ought not to stare at the screen for long periods of time.
2 You should/ought to avoid placing/You shouldn't/ought not to place the monitor so that it reflects a source of bright light, such as a window.
3 You should/ought to keep the screen clean to prevent distorting shadows.
4 If you work in an office with a large number of computers, you ought not to/you should not sit too close to the sides or backs of the monitors.
5 You should/ought to buy a protective filter that cuts down the ELF (extremely low frequency) emissions.

Unit 9 *Choosing a printer*

Topics
Types of printers
Advertisements for printers

Learning objectives
To understand the most important technical features of printers
To compare different types of printers
To recognize reference signals and linking devices (discourse cohesion)

Language
Grammar: Discourse cohesion: reference signals; linking devices
Revision of comparatives and superlatives
Vocabulary: Types of printers: *dot-matrix, ink-jet, bubble-jet, laser, thermal, imagesetter, plotter*

Other terms: *output, resolution, scalable fonts, dots per inch*
Abbreviations: *cps, SCSI*

Skills
Reading: Completing a table with technical information given in the text
Scanning advertisements
Listening: Listening to find out if statements are true or false
Writing: A paragraph describing the pros and cons of a particular printer
Speaking: Describing your ideal printer

Optional materials
Advertisements taken from mass media
A real printer from the computer classroom

Plan

Teacher's activities	Students' activities	Comments
1 Reading A Elicit some types of printers and write them on the board. B Pre-teach some key language: impact/non-impact, ink-jet, dot-matrix, etc. C You may like to write the table on the board and ask some SS to summarize the most important technical specifications. You can show SS some output examples in order to help them discriminate between different printing methods.	A SS make a list of the types of printers they think of, and read it aloud. B SS label the illustrations. C SS read through the text again and fill in the table. SS compare notes with a partner.	
2 Discourse cohesion A Emphasize the importance of pronouns and determiners as reference markers. C This activity is an opportunity to practise the use of linking devices. It could be given for homework.	Alone or in pairs, SS do **A** and **B**.	

3 Listening Ask SS to read the statements before listening. Check answers to **A** and **B** in whole-class feedback.	SS work individually, then compare answers with a partner. SS make the necessary changes to the false statements.	Some SS may find the task a bit difficult. Give them time to decide on their answers.
4 Scan reading: Quiz This is a competitive quiz, so you may like to set a reasonable time limit of 6–7 minutes. Ask for answers in class feedback.	In pairs, SS go through the adverts very quickly until they find the specific information they are looking for. After the quiz, they may read the adverts carefully.	
5 Language work: Revision of comparison **A** If necessary, explain particular rules of forming comparatives and superlatives. **B** Monitor the activity and help SS with structures and vocabulary.	SS do **A** and **B** and consolidate their knowledge of the use of comparatives and superlatives. SS work with a partner.	Explain the special cases *too slow/quick enough*, if the need arises.
6 Describing your ideal printer Encourage SS to be as creative as they like!		

Evaluation of the unit: ....
....

Answer key

1 Reading

A

Possible list of printers

dot-matrix, ink-jet, bubble-jet, laser, colour thermal printer, imagesetter, plotter

B
1. dot-matrix printer
2. ink-jet printer
3. laser printer
4. imagesetter
5. plotter

C

Type of printer	Technical specifications and other features
Dot-matrix	Uses pins to print low-resolution output; quality depends on the number of pins (9 or 24)
Ink-jet	Non-impact printer; projects ink droplets onto paper; some ink-jets produce high quality results; quite fast, silent
Laser	Scans the image with a laser beam, uses special ink powder; very high resolution; fast; scalable fonts and other advantages
Thermal	Uses heat, a special kind of paper and electrosensitive methods; silent; some colour models emulate HP plotters
Imagesetter	Prints on paper or microfilm; the highest resolution; very fast
Plotter	Uses ink and fine pens to draw detailed designs on paper

2 Discourse cohesion

A Reference signals

Line 1: **That** refers to 'printing' (anaphoric reference).
Line 3: **one** refers to which 'type of printer'.
Line 6: **such** qualifies the noun 'factors' specified by the following words 'noise or compatibility'.
Line 10: **They** refers to 'dot-matrix printers'.
Line 10: **them** refers to 'dot-matrix printers'.

B Linking devices

Indicating addition	Contrasting	Sequencing	Reason/ cause
and in addition	however while but nevertheless although	to begin with finally	since because

3 Listening

See tapescript in panel on page 38.

Tick statements 1, 4 and 5.
2 Ink-jet printers are more expensive than dot-matrix printers.
3 Ink-jet printers have become real competition for laser printers.
6 Ink-jets are ideal for individuals and small businesses.

4 Scan reading: Quiz

1 There are three laser printers.
2 Yes, the Colour Ink-Jet.
3 The Crystal Laser Printer II.
4 The Colour PostScript Printer (thermal method).
5 The Micro Laser XT or the Stylus Dot-matrix Printer.
6 The Crystal Laser Printer II.
7 Adobe PostScript and Hewlett Packard PCL.
8 One bi-directional parallel port, one LocalTalk port and one Ethernet port for networks.
9 dpi, cps, ppm, SCSI, LCD.

5 Language work: Revision of comparison

A

1 *cheaper than* ... Comparative; one-syllable adjective
2 *the fastest* ... Superlative; one-syllable adjective
3 *more expensive than* ... Comparative; polysyllabic adjective
4 *the most reliable of all.* Superlative; polysyllabic adjective
5 *cost less than ... also weigh less and require less space.* **Less** is a comparative adverb
6 *more resident fonts than* ... Comparative adjective; **more**+noun+**than**
7 *at a lower* ... Comparative; one-syllable adjective
8 *operate faster than* ... Comparative; one-syllable adverb
9 *too slow.* Special case: *too*+adj.
10 *not quick enough.* Special case: adj.+*enough*

Tapescript

Radio Presenter: Now it's time for this week's edition of *Hotline*, introduced by Miranda Green.

Miranda: Good morning. Are you about to buy a new printer? And are you confused about all the different sorts on the market? Well, this week we're looking at ink-jet and laser printers. In the studio with me is John Kelly from TexPrint, manufacturers of ink-jet printers. Mr Kelly, how does an ink-jet printer work?

Mr Kelly: Well, basically, an ink-jet printer operates by firing droplets of ink onto the paper.

Miranda: And is this a good method of printing?

Mr Kelly: Yes it is. It's much quieter than the dot-matrix printer and its output is of a much higher quality.

Miranda: But it's more expensive than the dot-matrix, isn't it?

Mr Kelly: It is, yes, but, as I say, it's quieter and produces better results.

Miranda: And what about laser printers? How do they compare with ink-jets?

Mr Kelly: Well, laser printers do produce better quality output than ink-jets, but ink-jets are still an excellent alternative and have become real competitors for laser printers.

Miranda: Why's that?

Mr Kelly: Well, they are much cheaper than laser printers and some of them can produce up to 720 dpi resolution, which is very good.

Miranda: And what kinds of things can ink-jets print? Can they just print sheets of paper, or do they do other things as well?

Mr Kelly: Oh yes, they can print envelopes, labels and even transparencies.

Miranda: And what about colour? Are there many colour ink-jet printers on the market?

Mr Kelly: There are indeed, and some are PostScript compatible, so they can be used in professional graphics and business presentations. They operate by mixing four inks – magenta, yellow, cyan and black – to produce different colours.

Miranda: What would your advice be to someone thinking about buying a printer?

Mr Kelly: Well, I think that a laser printer is the best option for workgroups and large businesses. Ink-jet printers are ideal for individuals and small businesses.

Miranda: Thank you very much, Mr Kelly.

PHOTOCOPIABLE © Cambridge University Press 2002

B

Possible answers (open task)

The Crystal Laser Printer II is faster than the Micro Laser XT but slower than the Turbo Laser Writer QR.

The Turbo Laser Writer QR has more internal fonts than the Micro Laser XT

The Micro Laser XT has less expandable RAM than the Turbo Laser Writer QR.

The Colour Ink-Jet is cheaper than the thermal colour printer (the Colour PostScript Printer).

The Thermal colour printer is more expensive than the laser printers.

A laser printer is better than a dot-matrix printer.

The Colour PostScript printer is the best of all; however, it is the most expensive.

Unit 10   *I/O devices for the disabled*

Topic
Adaptive technology for disabled people

Learning objectives
To understand what sort of input/output devices disabled people can use
To talk and write about how computers can be adapted for blind and motor-impaired users

Language
  Grammar: Noun phrases
  Range of modifiers: adjectives, participles, 's genitive, nouns
  Vocabulary: *Braille, speech synthesis system, magnification software, sip and puff, voice recognition system, on-screen keyboard, adaptive switch, eye-gaze system, touch screen,* etc.

Skills
  Speaking: Discussing problems faced by computer users with different disabilities and the kinds of devices which help to overcome these problems
  Reading: Reading to find specific information
  Listening: Taking notes
  Writing: A letter asking for information about computers for the disabled

Optional materials
Products designed for disabled computer users, or pictures of them

Internet work
Assistive technology

Plan

Teacher's activities	Students' activities	Comments
1 Adaptive technology Introduce the topic by directing SS' attention to the pictures. Question 1 can be split into two parts: (i) 'What difficulties do blind people have using a computer?'; (ii) 'What difficulties do people with limited mobility have?'	In pairs or small groups, SS describe the pictures and discuss the questions. They share their ideas with the rest of the class.	

2 Reading
  A Go round and help with difficult words or structures.
  B Check answers with the whole class.
	A SS work individually and then compare their answers in pairs.
	B SS do the matching exercise in pairs.
		This reading passage may be rather demanding for weaker students. Explain difficult terms (e.g. *emboss, virtual keyboard, sip and puff, eye-gaze system,* etc.).

3 Language work: Noun phrases Read through the grammar hints in the box with SS. Make sure they understand what a noun phrase is and the function and types of modifiers.		
4 Listening Read through the unfinished notes with the SS. You may need to pre-teach *expansion slot*.		

39

Play the interview all the way through and then let SS compare notes in pairs. Play the interview again, pausing after each question-and-answer if necessary. Ask them to check answers and complete notes. **5 Writing** If done in class, monitor SS' work and help where necessary.	SS listen and take notes. They compare notes in pairs. SS listen again, check their first answers and complete their notes. SS work alone (in class or at home).	

Evaluation of the unit: ....
....

Answer key

1 Adaptive technology

Here are some ideas

1 Of course, the main limitation experienced by blind users is the inability to see the screen. In addition, they cannot read printed documents, office correspondence, etc. Users with partial vision cannot see small character sizes on the screen.
There are various degrees of mobility limitation. Most motor-impaired users are not able to use a standard keyboard, and have difficulty in manipulating computer devices and printed material.
2 For blind users, devices include Braille input devices, speech synthesis systems, scanners (optical character recognition), Braille printers (embossers), etc.
3 There are adapted keyboards designed for people with different kinds of mobility limitations. There are a variety of alternative input devices that produce and transmit keystrokes as if generated by the keyboard. For example: muscle switches, optical head pointers, speech recognition devices, systems that scan the movements of the eye in order to make selections on the computer screen, etc.

2 Reading

A
1 Americans with Disabilities Act or *ADA*.
2 A screen magnification program.
3 Optical Character Recognition or *OCR*.
4 Pneumatic switch, also known as *sip and puff*.
5 Voice recognition systems understand human speech (they allow users to speak to the computer to input data).
6 They use a headset microphone, muscle switches and a joystick control.
7 He uses an adapted keyboard, headphones and screen reading software.
8 He uses an overlay keyboard operated by his feet.

B
a 2   b 3   c 5   d 1   e 4

3 Language work: Noun phrases

A
1 adjective   2 noun   3 's genitive
4 adjectives   5 participle   6 participle
7 noun

B
1 screen reader: A system that reads the screen.
2 printing devices: Devices that print.
3 company's database: The database that belongs to the company.
4 adapted keyboards: Keyboards that have been adapted (for special purposes).
5 magnification program: A program designed to magnify (text on the screen).
6 eye movements: Movements of the eye.

4 Listening

See tapescript in panel below.

A
- Work he's involved in: **A project for blind workers. Studying each person's needs and abilities; then designing and producing equipment for them**.
- Minimum configuration required to meet the needs of these workers:
  Processor: **800 MHz**
  RAM: **at least 256 MB**
- Expansion slots: **need five (for scanner, synthesizer, video and drive controllers, and one free)**
- Specific technologies (input/output devices): **Braille devices, speech synthesis systems, optical scanners, voice recognition devices**
- Companies that are developing adaptive equipment: **Compaq, Apple and IBM**

Tapescript

Interviewer: Can you tell me what kind of project you're working on at the moment?
Mike: Right now we're working with a group of blind workers. We're studying each person's needs and abilities, and then we're going to design and produce equipment for them.
Interviewer: What's the minimum configuration that you need to adapt a desktop computer for a blind person?
Mike: Both PCs and Macs need processors with 800 MHz of power to run many of the special applications, such as the optical character recognition or speech synthesis programs. The amount of RAM is also very important. Many adaptation programs require at least 256 MB.
Interviewer: And um … how many expansion slots would be needed?
Mike: It's really important to have enough expansion slots. If you have five, for example, you can install an optical scanner, a speech synthesizer, video and drive controllers, and still have a spare slot.
Interviewer: What sort of equipment do blind users find helpful?
Mike: Well, a blind person needs to interact with the computer in some way, and Braille devices and speech synthesis systems are very useful ways of enabling them to do this, as are optical scanners and voice recognition devices.
Interviewer: What's the difference between voice *recognition* devices and speech *synthesis* systems?
Mike: Well, voice recognition devices allow the user to instruct the computer verbally – with speech. Speech synthesis systems allow the computer to communicate with the user by reading the output from the screen in synthetic speech.
Interviewer: Which of the big companies are involved in producing these kinds of devices for blind users?
Mike: Compaq has DECtalk Express, a speech synthesizer which allows blind users to hear what is displayed on the screen. IBM has a speech recognition system called ViaVoice. And Apple has developed a lot of technologies for the blind; for example, CloseView, a screen magnification program, text-to-speech synthesis and talking alerts.
Interviewer: So blind users can look forward to more and better systems?
Mike: Yes, I think so.
Interviewer: Thank you very much for talking to us.
Mike: You're welcome.

PHOTOCOPIABLE © CAMBRIDGE UNIVERSITY PRESS 2002

Storage devices

Unit		page
11	*Magnetic drives*	43
12	*Optical breakthrough*	46

Unit 11   *Magnetic drives*

Topics
Floppies, hard disks, removables, DAT drives, microdrives
Formatting tracks and sectors

Learning objectives
To discriminate between different types of magnetic disks and drives
To give instructions and advice on how to protect data.

Language
Grammar: Instructions and advice: imperatives, *must/mustn't*
Vocabulary: *floppy, track, sector, format, magnetic, read/write head, directory, HD, hard drive, removable, cartridge, tape drive, pocket-sized drive, access time, data transfer rate, fragmentation, defragmentation,* etc.
Suffixes: *-ic, -ism, -ize, -ing, -er, -ation*

Skills
Reading: Understanding technical information
Listening: Listening for specific information
Speaking: Giving advice
Writing: Completing a text

Optional materials:
Real disks and drives (e.g. Zip, Jaz, etc.)

Plan

Teacher's activities	Students' activities	Comments
Section page You may like to ask some introductory questions like 'What are storage devices?', 'What do they do?'		
1 Types of drives You may like to show SS real examples of disks and drives. (Iomega is a popular manufacturer of removable drives.) Check answers with the whole class.	SS look at the illustrations and descriptions and find the required information. Then they compare answers in pairs.	In this unit, we study 'magnetic' drives. 'Optical' disks (CD-ROMs and DVDs) are discussed in Unit 12.
2 Listening Read the questions with the SS first. Then play the conversation. Check answers with the whole class.	SS work individually and then compare answers in pairs.	You may like to give them a copy of the tapescript (Buying a removable drive).
3 Protect your data **A** You can point out the form and use of imperatives here. **B** Explain the use of *must/mustn't*. This is an open task: you should avoid drilling.	**A** SS work individually, then check answers with a partner. **B** SS tell partner what he/she must/mustn't do to protect data.	You may like to point out the use of *should/shouldn't* to give advice (e.g. *You should keep all your disks in a safe place*).
4 Reading Emphasize that the diagram will help them understand the text.	SS read through the text, look at the diagram and in pairs do **A** and **B**. SS do **C** and give evidence from the text. *Optional*: SS correct the false statements.	Some SS may confuse **access time** with **data transfer rate**. Make sure they understand the difference. **Access time** – or **seek time** – refers to the amount

Unit 11 *Magnetic drives*

5 Word building Encourage SS to keep records of technical vocabulary according to word-building criteria (suffixes, prefixes and compounds).	SS choose the appropriate forms to complete the sentences.	of time it takes the hard disk to find the right sector where a given piece of data is stored. Access time is measured in milliseconds. **Data transfer rate** refers to the average speed required to transmit data from a disk system to the main memory. This is usually measured in megabits per second.

Evaluation of the unit: ....
....

Answer key

1 Types of drives

1 3.5 inches
2 1.44 megabytes
3 C drive
4 1.5 gigabytes
5 Digital Audio Tape (DAT) drive
6 Microdrive

2 Listening

See tapescript in panel.

1 Sue wants to buy a removable hard drive.
2 There are 100 MB and 250 MB Zip disks.
3 2 gigabytes
4 A Zip disk
5 £140
6 The Peerless

Tapescript

Assistant: £250. However, for that price you are getting a lot of power and memory.
Sue: Right. Thanks very much. I think I need to think about it.
Assistant: Fine. Do you want to take this catalogue?
Sue: Yes, thanks. Okay, bye.
Assistant: Bye.

PHOTOCOPIABLE © Cambridge University Press 2002

3 Protect your data

A

1 b   2 e   3 f   4 c   5 a   6 d

B
Possible answers
1 You must store them in a protective case. (Note: This is to keep dust off the disk and avoid corruption of data by accident.)
2 You must insert the disk into the disk drive very carefully.
3 You mustn't put disks near magnets. (Note: This is because magnetic fields corrupt data.)
4 You must update your anti-virus program regularly since new viruses are created everyday.
5 You must use passwords and security devices to protect confidential information.

4 Reading

A

1 c   2 d   3 f   4 e   5 a   6 b

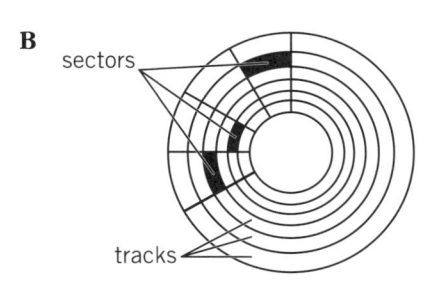

B

When a conventional disk is formatted, it is usually divided into 80 tracks, with 9 sectors per track in DD disks. (18 sectors per track in HD disks.)

C

1 T   2 T   3 F   4 T   5 T
6 F   7 F

5 Word building

magnet *noun*   magnetic *adjective*
magnetically *adverb*   magnetism *noun*
magnetize *verb*   magnetized *adjective*

1 Magnetism
2 magnetic
3 magnetized

record *verb*   recorder *noun*
recording *adjective*   recorded *verb* or *adjective*

4 recorded
5 recording
6 recorder

fragment *noun* or *verb*
fragmentation *noun*   defragmenter *noun*
fragmented *verb* or *adjective*

7 fragmented
8 Fragmentation
9 defragmenter

Unit 12 *Optical breakthrough*

Topic
CD-ROMs, DVD-ROMs and other forms of optical storage

Learning objectives
To develop reading skills by recognizing the most relevant information
To acquire technical vocabulary associated with optical storage devices

Language
Grammar: Reference signals
Connectors and modifiers
Vocabulary: *optical disk, optical drive*
Acronyms and abbreviations: *laser, ms, CD-ROM, CD-R, CD-RW, DVD-ROM, DVD-R*

Skills
Listening: Understanding the most relevant information
Reading: Identifying technical specs and use of particular optical disks
Analysing reference signals and linking words
Speaking: Discussing pros and cons of particular storage devices for different purposes

Optional materials
A CD-ROM disk, a DVD

Internet work
DVD technologies

Plan

Teacher's activities	Students' activities	Comments
1 Warm-up You can introduce the unit by showing a CD-ROM and then asking questions.	SS answer the questions (orally) and note any new vocabulary.	
2 Listening You may need to pre-teach words like *stamp, aluminium disk, laser beam, multimedia*.	SS read the sentences, listen and mark the incorrect ones. They listen again and rewrite the incorrect sentences.	
3 Reading Encourage SS to work out the meaning of unfamiliar words for themselves; explain only difficult terms. You may like to draw the table on the board and ask some SS to fill in the required information.	SS work individually. Then they compare notes with a partner.	CD-ROMs are 'read only' devices. However, today there are CD-RW (compact disk – rewritable) drives that can erase and rewrite CDs. DVD technology also uses different formats: DVD-ROM, DVD audio, DVD video, DVD-R and DVD-RW.
4 Discourse cohesion Explain that awareness of these elements of discourse can help SS develop their reading and writing skills in English.	SS work alone or in pairs.	This task highlights for SS how discourse is held together by reference signals, connectors and modifiers.

5 Speaking Check that SS understand how to use the expressions for giving opinions, expressing contrasts, agreeing and disagreeing. Tell them to give reasons for their choices.	In pairs or small groups, SS discuss the pros and cons of different storage devices.	Weaker students may need help with grammar and vocabulary.
6 Crossword	SS can do this at home, if required.	This reviews technical terms, synonyms, abbreviations and acronyms.

Evaluation of the unit: ....
....

Answer key

1 Warm-up

1 CD-ROM stands for 'compact disk read only memory'.
2 CD-ROM disks use optical technology. The data is retrieved using a laser beam.

2 Listening

See tapescript in panel below.

Sentences with mistakes: 1, 2, 4, 5, 7
1 A CD-ROM disk is like a compact music disk. (The only difference is that instead of holding music, it holds computer information.)
2 You need an optical drive (a CD-ROM player) to read CD-ROM disks.
4 A typical CD-ROM disk can hold 650 MB.
5 The data on a CD-ROM cannot be changed or 'written' to.
7 CD-ROM drives can play audio CDs.

Tapescript

Paul: Can you tell me what a CD-ROM disk is, exactly?
Assistant: Well, it's just the same as a CD used for music, only instead of music it stores computer information. The data is stamped onto the aluminium disk which is then covered in plastic.
Paul: And do you need a special drive to read one?
Assistant: Yes, you need a CD-ROM drive, which reads the data with a laser beam.
Paul: And how much information is on each disk?
Assistant: Masses! A typical CD-ROM disk can hold 650 megabytes of sound, text, photographs, music, multimedia material and applications.
Paul: Gosh! And can you add your own material to what's on the disk?
Assistant: No, you can't – it's like a music CD – you can't change what's on there. It's not designed for you to write on – it's designed to hold lots of information that the user doesn't need to change.
Paul: And can you use a CD-ROM drive to play CDs on?
Assistant: Yeah, on most CD-ROM drives. If you come with me I'll show you what drives we've got …

PHOTOCOPIABLE © Cambridge University Press 2002

3 Reading

	Technical specifications	*Use*
CD-ROM	Can store a lot of information (650 MB) Economical way of sharing information Can't write anything to it	Used to store software, dictionaries, multimedia databases, etc. Can play music CDs
CD-Recorder	Allows you to create CDs in a format that can be read by a CD-R drive or a regular CD-ROM drive. Come in two different forms: CD-R (recordable) and CD-RW (rewritable)	To back up hard disks or to distribute and archive information
DVD	A DVD-ROM can hold 17 GB, about 25 times an ordinary CD-ROM. It's a 'read-only' device. There are also DVD rewritable drives	To store multimedia software and complete Hollywood movies Can also play music CDs and CD-ROMs
Magneto-optical	Uses both a laser and an electromagnet to record information MO disks are rewritable	Ideal for back-up and portable mass storage

4 Discourse cohesion

A Reference signals

1 (line 6) **they** refers to optical disks
2 (line 23) **which** refers to the fact that one CD can replace 300,000 pages of text (about 500 floppies)
3 (line 27) **you** has an indefinite usage here, meaning 'people in general'. The use of *you* is informal, often preferred to *one*, which is formal.
4 (line 29) **it** refers to a CD-ROM disk
5 (line 50) **both** refers to the two – a laser and an electromagnet

B Connectors and modifiers

a Showing contrast: *However, Yet*
b Explaining causes and results: *Thus, For this reason*
c Adding new ideas: *Besides, In addition*

5 Speaking

Suggested answers

1 A hard disk
2 A tape drive or a removable cartridge drive
3 A CD-ROM
4 An erasable optical disk system
5 A Digital Video Disk-ROM

6 Crossword

	¹L	A	²S	E	R				³H		⁴P	⁵C
	A				⁶R	E	C	O	R	D		A
	N				A				C			R
⁸F		⁹W		¹⁰S	T	O	R	¹¹E		¹²B	I	T
O		O		A				X				R
R		R		B		¹³D		P				I
M		¹⁴M	I	L	L	I	S	E	C	O	N	D
¹⁵A	T			E		S		N			¹⁶H	
T						K		S			H	E
¹⁷T	R	A	C	K		¹⁸G	I	G	A			
E						¹⁹C		V		²⁰R	O	²¹M
²²D	R	I	V	E				E		D		B

48

Basic software

Unit		page
13	*Operating systems*	50
14	*The graphical user interface*	53
15	*A walk through word processing*	56
16	*Spreadsheets*	59
17	*Databases*	62
18	*Faces of the Internet*	65

Unit 13 *Operating systems*

Topics
　Software: operating systems
　System utilities

Learning objectives
　To understand the function of operating systems
　To extract specific information from oral and written texts about system software
　To learn the terminology and utilities associated with operating systems
　To use the correct determiners with countable and uncountable nouns

Language
　Grammar: Countable and uncountable nouns
　Vocabulary: *system software, operating system, applications programs, multitasking, utility*
　System utilities: *virus detector, screen saver, multimedia player, crashed disk rescuer*

Skills
　Reading: Extracting specific information from a text
　Listening: Identifying different types of system utilities from advertisements

Internet work
　Computer viruses

Plan

Teacher's activities	Students' activities	Comments
Section page You may want to point out the learning objectives to SS. You could also ask them to make a list of different types of software.	SS familiarize themselves with the topics and objectives of the section.	
1 Warm-up **A** Talk through the diagram with the SS and ask for answers to the question.	**A** It is assumed that SS have heard of operating systems before. The diagram will help them explain the purpose of the OS.	
B Make sure they understand the difference between *operating system* and *applications software*. Check answers with the whole class.	**B** SS work alone to complete the text with the phrases.	
2 Reading You may need to explain some of the vocabulary.	SS read the text and find the required information. They can work in pairs.	There are other 'non-mainstream' operating systems. (E.g. BeOS, EPOC, Windows CE)
3 Language work Direct SS' attention to the HELP box. Provide some other examples about the use of determiners with countable and uncountable nouns. Present typical mistakes on the board.	SS first study the HELP box. Then they do **A–C** individually. Finally, SS should check their answers.	A contrastive analysis with mother tongue may be useful.

4 Listening

Before listening, ask SS to read the box.
Encourage them to use the Glossary.
Make sure they understand the purpose of system utilities: these are small programs which improve the performance of the OS.

A SS read the instructions and the information in the box. They may need to look up the meaning of *utility*, *virus* and *screen saver* in the Glossary. SS listen and number the utilities in the order they hear them.

B SS listen again and decide which utility is most appropriate for each situation. They then compare answers with a partner.

Evaluation of the unit: ....
....

Answer key

1 Warm-up

A
Possible answers
The function of the operating system is to control the hardware and software resources.
The operating system consists of a set of programs that interface between the user, applications programs and the computer. (Note: The OS translates commands into machine code that the computer understands.)

B
1 software   2 system software
3 applications software   4 operating system

2 Reading

1 MS-DOS (Microsoft Disk Operating System).
2 Windows XP
3 Microsoft Pocket PC OS
4 The function of the Finder is to display the Macintosh's desktop and to enable the user to work with disks, programs and files.
5 'Multitasking' means that several programs are executed (and various tasks done) at the same time.
6 UNIX
7 Linux
8 Solaris

3 Language work: Countable and uncountable nouns

A

Countable	Uncountable
window	robotics
program	hacking
hacker	hardware
system	software
workstation	

B
1 We are having terrible weather.
2 Can you give me some advice?
3 I need some information.
4 The news was very depressing.
5 I like the furniture.
6 Many people use the Web today.

C
1 a   2 the   3 -   4 -   5 an
6 -   7 the   8 -   9 -   10 an

4 Listening

See tapescript in panel on page 52.

Tapescript

1 Worried about computer viruses? Afraid that one could invade your system and delete your files or destroy the contents of your hard disk? Don't worry. With Antidote, the new virus detector from MCC, you can use disks with confidence. Antidote scans all disks, locates and destroys any viruses and will also eradicate any existing infections. Antidote – your only choice in virus protection.

2 Computer screens need protecting. If the same image remains on your screen for a long time, it can be burnt onto it and remain as a permanent ghost image. To stop this happening, you can use ScreenShapes, a new and inexpensive program that will darken the screen automatically and display all sorts of animated patterns if the screen is left unused for three minutes. Available from your local computer centre now for only £9.

3 Would you like to have just one program for all your multimedia activities? What you need is Media Wizard – a utility that lets you watch video and DVDs, listen to radio stations on the Internet, play MP3 music and burn your CDs. It's like having radio, a CD player, and a movie organizer in a single program. Media Wizard, the best player for your media collection!

4 Oh no! You're having another crisis with your computer! You've accidently deleted a file or reformatted a disk that you wanted to keep. What can you do? With DiskRescue there's no need to panic. DiskRescue is a utility which will repair hard and floppy disks, restore deleted files and even recover corrupted files that refuse to open. Make an appointment with DiskRescue today to ensure the health of your disks.

PHOTOCOPIABLE © Cambridge University Press 2002

A
1 virus detector
2 screen saver
3 multimedia player
4 crashed disk rescuer and data recovery

B
1 multimedia player
2 crashed disk rescuer and data recovery
3 screen saver
4 virus detector (anti-virus program)

Notes
- Utilities are used by the system to do various tasks more easily and faster.
- System utilities include anti-virus programs, printing aids, font movers, back-up utilities, disk repair programs, screen savers, file finders, etc.
- A virus is a piece of software which attaches itself to another file or application. Some viruses can delete files or destroy the contents of hard disks. The function of an anti-virus program is to scan, find and destroy viruses.

Unit 14 *The graphical user interface*

Topic	Skills
The graphical user interface	**Reading:** Getting the general idea of an article
Learning objectives	Guessing the meaning of words from the context
To recognize the characteristics of a typical graphical user interface or GUI	**Listening:** Completing a fact file about Microsoft Windows
To learn how to summarize a written text	**Writing:** Summarizing a written text
Language	**Optional materials**
Grammar: Ways of reducing sentences	A system with a user interface based on graphics, e.g. Windows, Macintosh or IBM OS/2 Warp
Vocabulary: *window box, scroll bar, icon, pull-down menu, pointer, user-friendly, folder,* etc.	**Internet work**
	A virtual interface

Plan

Teacher's activities	Students' activities	Comments
1 A user-friendly interface Read through the task and box with SS. Explain that the illustration shows a Macintosh screen with various interface elements. Check answers with the whole class. *Option:* You may like to show the SS a graphical environment on the computer.	SS find the different interface elements in the illustration.	This task is designed to illustrate the elements of a user interface based on graphics and to prepare SS for reading.
2 Reading A Ask SS to read the passage once in order to get a general idea of the content. B Encourage SS to guess the meaning of the vocabulary from the context; explain some of it if necessary. C Check answers with the whole class.	A SS read the article and decide which of the expressions best describe a GUI. B SS try to guess the meaning of some key words. C Alone or in pairs, SS find the specific information needed to answer the questions.	
3 Listening Pre-teach some words from the fact file and the sample screen.	SS read the fact file and look at the sample screen from Windows. They listen to the cassette and complete the fact file. Then they compare their answers in pairs. SS listen again and check their answers.	There are more activities about Microsoft Windows on the Infotech website.

Unit 14 *The graphical user interface*

4 Writing	
(This can be set as homework if you are short of time.) Read the steps aloud and explain where necessary. Check SS understand the different ways of reducing sentences.	SS follow the step-by-step instructions and summarize the text in 70–75 words. They can write the final version at home.

Evaluation of the unit: ....
....

Answer key

1 A user-friendly interface

1 window: area showing the contents of Macintosh HD.

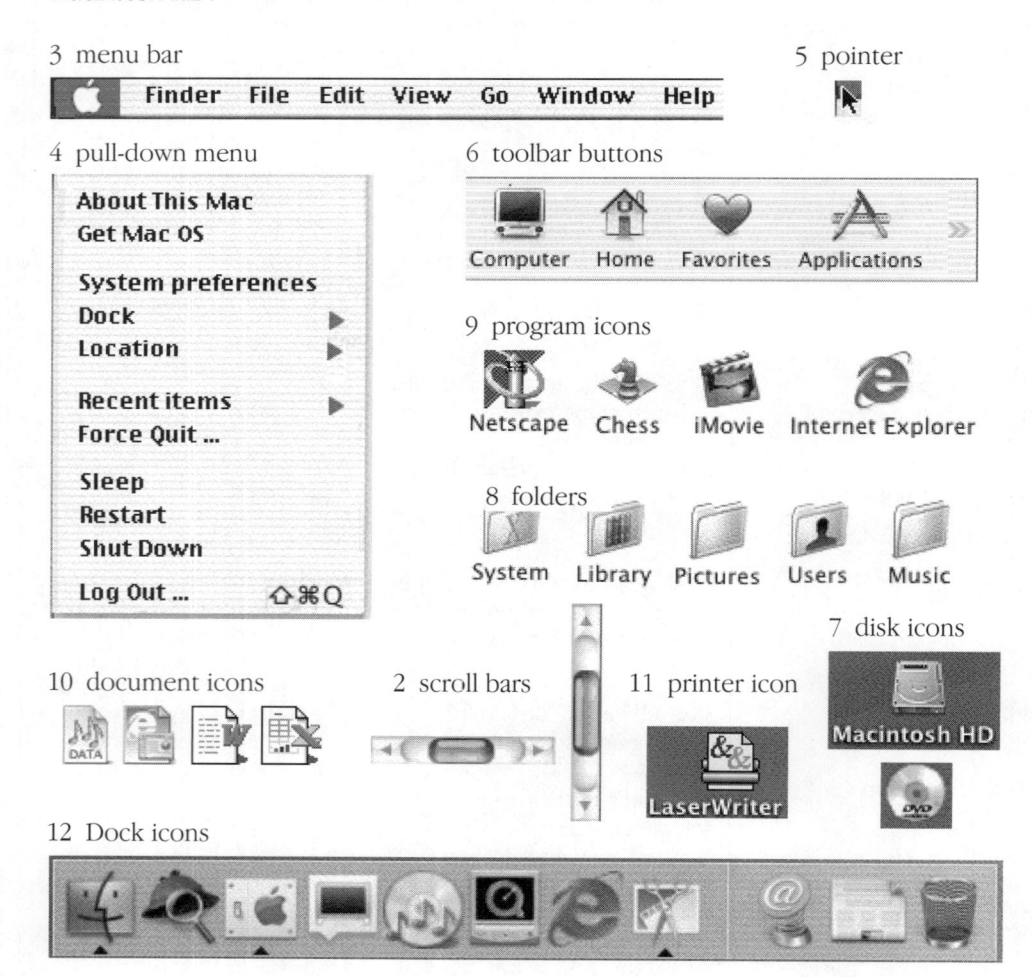

3 menu bar

5 pointer

4 pull-down menu

6 toolbar buttons

9 program icons
Netscape   Chess   iMovie   Internet Explorer

8 folders
System   Library   Pictures   Users   Music

7 disk icons

10 document icons   2 scroll bars   11 printer icon

12 Dock icons

> **Tapescript**
>
> Interviewer: There's no doubt that Windows has revolutionized the way we use PCs today. Can you explain why this system is so popular?
>
> Bill: Well, people find this system very easy to use because everything is presented in graphic images. It's compatible with thousands of programs, and allows multi-tasking.
>
> Interviewer: And how many types of Windows systems are there?
>
> Bill: Well, the Windows family covers almost all computing platforms. Older versions like Windows 98 and Windows 2000 have been replaced by the new Windows XP. This operating system comes in two versions: The Windows XP Home Edition and The Windows XP Professional. The Home Edition is ideal for home users. The Professional version is aimed at business users.
>
> Interviewer: Right. And what other factors make Windows so attractive?
>
> Bill: The user interface has been redesigned with a new visual style, and the system offers support for the latest technologies, from digital cameras to DVDs. It also includes Windows Media Player, a program that lets you download, play and organize your music CDs and videos.
>
> Interviewer: Really? And what about Internet connections, have they been improved?
>
> Bill: Yes, Internet Explorer is more reliable and secure. The browser is integrated into the operating system, so you can search files and folders on your hard disk, surf the Web or find pages on your company intranet. The system also has a Connection Firewall that protects your computer from Internet attacks.
>
> Interviewer: And what sort of applications can you use with Windows?
>
> Bill: The most popular is Microsoft Office, a suite that includes a word processor, an e-mail program, a spreadsheet program called Excel, and a presentation graphics program known as PowerPoint.
>
> Interviewer: Thanks very much.
>
> **PHOTOCOPIABLE**   © CAMBRIDGE UNIVERSITY PRESS 2002

2 Reading

A

user-friendly; attractive; graphics-based

C

1 'GUI' stands for 'graphical user interface'.
2 From the first, Macintosh computers had a user-friendly interface based on graphics and intuitive tools: pull-down menus, windows, icons, dialog boxes, mouse, pointer, etc.
3 'WIMP' stands for Window, Icon, Menu (or Mouse) and Pointer.
4 The Macintosh environment, Microsoft Windows and IBM OS/2 Warp
5 By double-clicking its icon.
6 Graphical user interfaces are easy to use – you don't need to memorize complex commands. They stimulate users to be more creative.

3 Listening

See tapescript in panel above.

1 easy to use
2 compatible
3 The Windows XP Home Edition
4 The Windows XP Professional
5 Media Player
6 Internet attacks
7 Microsoft Office

4 Writing

Possible answer

In the past, only experts used computers. Nowadays, however, many people have access to computers, so there is an emphasis on the user interface.

Macintosh computers were designed on a WIMP interface to facilitate the user's interaction with the computer. Other innovative GUIs are MS Windows and IBM OS/2 Warp.

Unit 15 A walk through word processing

Topic
Word processors

Learning objectives
To understand the basic features and applications of word processors
To compare word-processing capabilities

Language
Grammar: Sequencers: *first, now, next, finally*
Vocabulary: *edit, format, search, replace, indent, WYSIWYG, clipboard, header, footer, mail merging, spell checker, online thesaurus, grammar checker,* etc.

Skills
Reading: Looking for specific information
Listening: Checking for predicted answers in gap-filling activity
Writing: Describing the 'Cut and Paste' technique
Speaking: Comparing word processors

Optional materials
A word processor on the computer

Plan

Teacher's activities	Students' activities	Comments
1 Before you read If you have access to a word processor (e.g. MS Word, WordPerfect), you can introduce the theme by showing the program on a computer. You can go through the questions with the whole class. Alternatively, ask SS to work in small groups and to prepare an oral report.	SS answer the questions and familiarize themselves with the theme of the unit. Alternatively, each group prepares an oral report for the class.	
2 Reading **A** Go round and help with new vocabulary. You may like to comment on the sample screen. **B** and **C** Give SS a few minutes to do these. Check they understand basic terminology.	**A** SS read through the text and underline those facilities they did not mention in Task 1. **B** and **C** SS complete the sentences and then match the words and expressions.	
3 Listening Direct SS' attention to the time sequences in the box. You may want to ask them to read the conversation aloud in pairs. Ask them to look at the Edit menu and to translate the commands into their own language.	First, SS read through the conversation and complete it with words from the box. Then they listen and check their predictions. SS read the Edit menu and give equivalent commands in their own language.	

4 Writing If you don't have enough time, set this task for homework.	Using the picture, SS write a short description of the 'Cut and Paste' process.	
5 Writing tools Set **A** and **B** at the same time. Check answers with the whole class.	SS look at the windows or dialog boxes, read through the texts and do the task.	This will help SS to learn about three writing tools: a spell checker, an online thesaurus and a grammar checker.
6 Speaking Give SS time to read the table of characteristics. Before they start speaking, focus on useful expressions and on the pronunciation of specific items.	In pairs, SS build up a conversation. They try to convince their partners of the advantages of their respective programs.	Weaker SS may have some difficulties in managing conversations. This is a good opportunity to practise communicative strategies.

Evaluation of the unit: ....
....

Answer key

1 Before you read

Possible answers

1 A word processor is a computer program which manipulates texts (and produces documents suitable for printing).
2 With a word processor you can:
   - change the text as often as you want before printing the final document (you don't have to retype it all)
   - edit on-screen, move text around, insert new text, delete unnecessary text, etc. Doing all this with a typewriter requires constant marking and retyping of drafts because you are typing directly on paper.
3 Features offered by word processors:
   - Editing: copy, cut, paste and delete text and graphics
   - Search and Replace
   - Formatting (automatic page numbering, headers and footers, justification, footnotes and endnotes, multiple columns)
   - viewing hidden commands in the text
   - typestyles like bold and italic, super- and subscript characters
   - running text and graphics
   - automatic hyphenation
   - spell checker
   - mail merging
   - tables, indexes, tables of contents
   - borders.

2 Reading

B

1 WYSIWYG   2 Justification
3 font menu   4 Type style (×2)
5 format   6 Mail merging   7 indent (×2)

C

1 b   2 f   3 a   4 d   5 c   6 e

3 Listening

A

1 First   2 command   3 now
4 insertion   5 Next   6 Edit
7 Finally   8 mistake

4 Writing

Possible answer

The picture is a visual representation of the 'Cut and Paste' editing technique. By using these commands you can move text (or graphics) within a document, between documents or between programs.

First, select the portion of text that you want to move. Then, choose Cut from the Edit menu, and the selected text disappears and is placed on the Clipboard – temporary storage inside the computer. Next, scroll to the new position and click to insert the cursor. Finally, choose Paste from the Edit menu; this inserts the content of the Clipboard into the active document at the insertion point.

5 Writing tools

A

1 c   2 a   3 b

B

1 'Like a conventional thesaurus, this database of words contains definitions and suggestions of words with similar and opposite meanings' should appear in text 2 after the first sentence.
2 'Their power comes not from knowing every grammatical rule, but from questioning the writer about certain parts of the text' should appear in text 3 after the fourth sentence.
3 'However, this does not mean that all of the words in the document are spelled correctly' should appear in text 1 after the second sentence.

Unit 16 *Spreadsheets*

Topic
The form and function of spreadsheet programs

Learning objectives
To understand the basic features of spreadsheets
To acquire specific vocabulary connected with spreadsheet programs

Language
Vocabulary: *column, row, cell, formula, value, pie chart, sales, share, interest, revenue, income, payroll, salary, services, expenses, amount, VAT, subtotal, net profits, invoice, bill, account, to borrow, to invest,* etc.

Skills
Listening: Listening for specific and general information
Speaking: Answering questions about spreadsheets and visual representations
Writing: Producing an invoice

Optional materials
Working with a real spreadsheet program

Plan

Teacher's activities	Students' activities	Comments
1 Looking at a spreadsheet You may like to introduce the unit by showing the SS a spreadsheet program on a computer. Ask them to compare its presentation with the illustration in their Student's Book. Optional warm-up questions: 'Have you ever used a spreadsheet? What for?'	SS look at the spreadsheet and answer the questions orally.	
2 Listening **B** Ask SS to justify their answers. You can ask them to correct the false statements. Check answers with the whole class.	**A** SS listen and check their answers to Task 1. **B** SS read the statements, listen again and decide which ones are right or wrong.	The passage might be a bit difficult for some SS, but the task is easy. If necessary, let them read the tapescript.
3 Vocabulary Write the words on the blackboard and practise their pronunciation. Set the task. You may need to explain the meaning of some words (e.g. *borrow, invest, loan, amount, wages*).	SS practise the pronunciation of the words in the box. Then they match the words with the dictionary-type explanations.	

4 Graphic representation Go round and help SS with vocabulary or mathematical problems. Check answers and discuss **D** with the whole class. You may like to ask SS to generate a spreadsheet and a corresponding chart on a computer. Offer them various themes: income tax, pocket money, the school budget, etc.	SS can work in pairs to do **A** to **C** and to discuss **D**.	
5 Extension **A** Explain the difference between *bill* and *invoice*. **B** You may want to set this for homework.	**A** SS look at the invoice and fill in the blanks with the right words. **B** If possible, they generate a similar invoice outside class.	To do **B**, SS need a program like MS Excel or Lotus 1-2-3. This can be set as an optional mini-project.

Evaluation of the unit: ....
....

Answer key

1 Looking at a spreadsheet

1 A spreadsheet is like a large sheet of paper with a lot of columns and rows. It is used in business for financial planning: to make specific calculations, keep a record of the company's accounts, etc.
2 'Columns' are the vertical divisions of the spreadsheet. Each column is labelled with a letter, for example, A, B, C. 'Rows' are the lines, i.e. the horizontal divisions of the spreadsheet. They are labelled with numbers.
3 You can enter text, numbers and formulas (or formulae).
4 The values of the spreadsheet are automatically recalculated.

2 Listening

See tapescript in panel on page 61.

B
1 right   2 wrong   3 wrong   4 right
5 wrong

C
6 right   7 wrong   8 right

3 Vocabulary

1 g   2 b   3 c   4 f   5 e
6 h   7 a   8 d

4 Graphic representation

A The graph *is* a visual representation of the spreadsheet illustrated in Task 1.
B Net profits of this firm during the period 2001–2002: 339–172 = $167,000,000
C Bar chart
D From the graph the reader can immediately compare the 2001 and 2002 figures and can also compare the different kinds of revenue and expenses.

Tapescript

A spreadsheet program is normally used in business for financial planning – to keep a record of accounts, to analyse budgets or to make specific calculations. It's like a large piece of paper divided into columns and rows. Each column is labelled with a letter and each row is labelled with a number. The point where a column and a row intersect is called a cell. For example, you can have cells A1, B6, C5, and so on.

A cell can hold three types of information: text, numbers and formulas. For example, in the sample spreadsheet, the word *sales* has been keyed into cell A2 and the values 890, 487 and 182 have been entered into cells B2, B3 and B4 respectively. So when the formula 'B2 + B3 + B4' is keyed into cell B5 the program automatically calculates and displays the result.

Formulas are functions or operations that add, subtract, multiply or divide existing values to produce new values. We can use them to calculate totals, percentages or discounts.

When you change the value of one cell, the values in other cells are automatically recalculated. You can also update the information in different worksheets by linking cells. This means that when you make a change in one worksheet the same change is made in the other worksheet.

The format menu in a spreadsheet usually includes several commands allowing you to choose the font, number alignment, borders, column width and so on.

Most spreadsheet programs can generate documents with graphic representations and some include three-dimensional options. The values of cells are shown in different ways such as line graphs, bar or pie charts.

Some programs also have a database facility which transforms the values of the cells into a database. In this case each column is a field and each row is a record.

PHOTOCOPIABLE © Cambridge University Press 2002

5 Extension

A

Name:	Redwood Comprehensive School			
Address	Springbank Road, Easthill		**Invoice**	
Telephone:	436171		Date:	12 March 2003

Reference	Description	Qty	Price	Total
Ulysses Classic	256 MB of RAM, 60 GB HD	12	£ 1,050	£ 12,600
XGA Monitor	Colour 16"	9	225	2,025
Video Card	Millions of colours	5	316	1,580
Portable Ulysses	128 MB RAM, 40 GB HD	3	1,190	3,570
Laser SAT	PostScript	1	825	825
Scanner JUP	Flatbed. Includes OCR	2	675	1,350
			Subtotal	£ 21,950
			VAT 17.5%	3,841
Company			TOTAL	£ 25,791
Ulysses Computers, Inc.				

Unit 17 *Databases*

Topics	Skills
Database programs Mail merging **Learning objectives** To understand the basic features and applications of a database To learn specific vocabulary associated with database software **Language** **Grammar:** plurals **Vocabulary:** *database, field, record, layout, sort, update, mail merging*, etc.	**Reading:** Selecting main features of a database Guessing the meaning of new words from the context **Listening:** Understanding instructions **Writing:** A standard letter offering new software products to several clients **Optional materials** A real database program

Plan

Teacher's activities	Students' activities	Comments
1 Warm-up Use the illustrations to illustrate the difference between the terms *file*, *record* and *field*. These terms are needed for the next task. *Option:* You may like to introduce the lesson by showing the SS a database program on the computer. **2 Reading** B Remind SS that guessing meaning from context is a useful strategy which will help them expand their vocabulary. C Check answers with the whole class. **3 Puzzle** **4 Language work: Plurals** Refer SS to the grammar box and make sure they understand the plural forms and the pronunciation of the 's'.	SS study the illustrations and try to answer the questions. A First SS work alone, underlining the main ideas. Then they confer in pairs. B SS make a list of words/ expressions they don't understand, and practise guessing their meaning. C SS complete the statements with the information from the text. In pairs, SS complete the sentences and the crossword.	 This task recycles vocabulary connected with databases. Some SS may find it difficult to discriminate between the voiceless /s/ and the voiced /z/.

Ask them to do **A** to **C**. Then play the cassette so that SS can check their answers to **C**. You may like to write Activity **C** on the board. **5 Listening** **A** Explain the terms *mail* and *merge* (combine two files together to make one). **B** Draw SS' attention to the illustration of the mail merging technique. **6 Writing** You can set this task as homework. *Option:* If SS have access to a computer, ask them to write a personalized version of the letter to several clients.	SS study the grammar box and do parts **A** to **C**. Then they listen and check their pronunciation. **A** SS listen and number the instructions in the correct order. **B** SS study the illustration and identify the three types of documents involved in mail merging. Individually, SS write a standard letter. *Option:* Working in pairs or small groups, SS practise mail merging on the computer.	The /ɪz/ sound should not represent a problem. You could add some other examples: *gases, classes, dishes, churches, houses.* *Option:* To carry out this mini-project, SS will need a computer and appropriate software.

Evaluation of the unit: ....
....

Answer key

1 Warm-up

Possible answers

1 A database is:
   - a file of structured data
   - a large collection of related information
   - an organized collection of data stored in a computer file.
2 Possible applications
   - To keep personal records or mailing lists with names, addresses, phone numbers, salaries, departments, etc.
   - To keep track of stock, sales, orders, bills and other financial information.
   - To store and find information about patients in a hospital or general medical practice.
   - To keep records of students/pupils at college/school.

3 (Note: For example, a *file* might contain the personnel records of a company. The *record* shown here holds information about one employee. Each piece of information in a record is given a separate *field*: for example, the 'name' is a field.)

2 Reading

C

1 A database is used to **store, organize and retrieve a large collection of related information**.
2 Information is entered on a database via **fields**.
3 Each field holds **a separate piece of information**.
4 'Updating' a file means **making changes, adding new records or deleting old ones**.
5 The advantages of a database program over a manual filing system are:
   - **it is much faster to consult**
   - **it occupies much less space**
   - **records can be easily sorted**

- **information can be easily updated**
- **computer databases can be shared by a lot of users on a network**.

6 Access to a common database can be protected by using **security devices such as passwords**.

3 Puzzle

	1 M	E	R	G	I	N	G
		2 S	O	R	T	E	D
3 R	E	C	O	R	D		
		4 U	P	D	A	T	E	D
5 D	A	T	A	B	A	S	E
		6 L	A	Y	O	U	T
			7 F	I	E	L	D

4 Language work: Plurals

A
1 slots 2 keys 3 directories
4 businessmen 5 faxes 6 mice
7 floppies 8 viruses

B
invoices, packages, facilities, businesses, devices

C

/s/	/ɪz/	/z/
laptops	images	passwords
budgets	taxes	fields
graphics	expenses	folders
disks	interfaces	pixels

5 Listening

See tapescript in panel.

A

1 Create the data document with a database program or with the right spreadsheet software. This document contains rows with names, addresses and other information that will be merged with the standard letter.

2 Create the main document with a word processor. Type the standard letter and insert the appropriate field names into it.
3 Activate the Mail Merge command (Print Merge in some programs). This combines the main document and the data document.
4 Click 'Print' and the program generates a single letter for each record in the data document.

B

The three types of documents involved in the example of mail merging are: (i) the data document; (ii) the main document (the standard letter); and (iii) the personalized versions of the letter (multiple copies of the main document) generated after merging the two previous documents.

Tapescript

If you want to personalize a standard letter you can use 'mail merging', which is a technique that combines a database file with a standard letter typed on a word processor.

To merge the file with the letter you have to do four things.

First you create the data document with a database program or with a spreadsheet which has database facilities. This document contains the fields and the information that will vary in each version of the letter. Save this in a format that a word processor can understand.

After this, create the standard letter and include in it where you want the information from the database to go. You do this by putting in the field names from the data document.

Then activate the Mail Merge or Print Merge command in the File menu of the word processor. This combines the two documents.

Finally, just click the appropriate Print button and you will get personalized versions of the standard letter.

PHOTOCOPIABLE © Cambridge University Press 2002

Unit 18 *Faces of the Internet*

Topic
 Internet sofware
 Internet applications

Learning objectives
 To understand how the Internet works
 To recognize the basic features of the Web
 To acquire specific vocabulary related to e-mail and other Internet services

Language
 Grammar: *be going to* + infinitive
 Vocabulary: *modem, e-mail, @, file transfer, real-time chat, web browser, newsgroup, Internet telephone, intranet, Telnet, website, web address, search, link, attachment, video conferencing*
 Abbreviations: *ISP, IRC, FTP, TCP/IP, PPP, HTML, URL*

Skills
 Listening: Completing notes
 Reading: Understanding general and specific information about Internet software
 Speaking: Participating in an imaginary chat session
 Writing: Replying to an e-mail message

Optional materials
 Working with a Web browser and a mail program
 Taking printed web pages to class

Internet work
 History of the Internet

Plan

Teacher's activities	Students' activities	Comments
1 Get ready for listening Encourage SS to talk about the Internet and its applications. Draw their attention to the sample screen of Internet Explorer. You may like to pre-teach *modem, Internet service provider, Web browser, online chat, file transfer*	Using the picture and their own knowledge, SS brainstorm ideas about the questions.	
2 Listening There may be some SS in your classroom that have access to the Internet, so you can ask them questions like: 'Do you have an Internet account? How much do you pay per month? What do you use the Web for?'	SS listen and complete the notes. Then they compare answers with a partner.	Some SS, particularly those that have never used the Internet, may have comprehension problems. Let them use the Glossary and make sure they understand basic concepts (what you need to telecommunicate, Internet services, the Web).

3 Reading
  A Make sure SS distinguish the function of the different Internet tools. Ask them which of these software utilities they have used.
  B Go round and help with difficult words or structures. In class feedback, ask for evidence for their answers from the text.
	A SS decide which Internet tool they would use to do the tasks. Then they read the text and check their answers.
	B SS read the text again and choose the correct definition for specific technical terms.	

Unit 18 *Faces of the Internet*

4 Speaking
  A You may like to ask SS if they use an 'instant message' service to chat with friends.
  B Draw SS' attention to the sample screen and explain that IRC is conducted by typing messages at the keyboard. Ask them to act the dialogue. Revise the use of *be going to* if necessary.

5 A typical Web page
  A Read through the task, HELP box and screen shot with SS.
  B If SS have access to the Internet, you may like to ask them to search for information about a certain topic, e.g. 'Planning a trip'.

6 Writing
  A Write some e-mail addresses on the board and explain the format. Examples:
  president @ whitehouse.gov
  jbrown@ednet.co.uk
  Iwain@aol.com
  The domain name indicates the type of organization: *.com* for commercial (*.co* in the UK), *.edu* for education, *.gov* for government, *.org* for organization, etc.
  B Monitor the writing activity. Help them with words and grammar.

A SS ask and answer the questions in pairs.
B SS first complete the dialogue. Then, in pairs, they act out the conversation.

A SS identify the basic features of a web page and learn the format of a web address.
B SS choose the most suitable web address for the requirements.

A SS learn the format of an e-mail address and identify the parts of a message.

B SS reply to the e-mail message.

Online chatting includes various technologies: IRC, audio and video chatting, virtual reality worlds. In a program like *Worlds Chat*, participants are represented by characters called avatars (persons, fish, insects, etc.).

Notes:
The line Cc: in an e-mail program means carbon copy. The line Bcc: means blind carbon copy. See the list of abbreviations.

Evaluation of the unit: ....
....

Answer key

1 Get ready for listening

1 The Internet is a global network of computer networks. It allows organizations and individuals to share all sorts of information and computer resources.
2 You can send and receive e-mail, explore the Web, transfer files, have live conversations, take part in online forums, use remote computers, etc. You can use the Web to:
  • find and download software
  • buy products online
  • search for information
  • read information about thousands of topics.

2 Listening

See tapescript in panel on page 67.
1 modem
2 computer
3 telephone line
4 communications port
5 telephone line
6 service provider
7 e-mail
8 file transfer
9 newsgroup
10 real-time chats
11 World Wide Web
12 pages

Tapescript

Journalist: Everybody says the Internet is really exciting. But what exactly is the Internet?

Mr Morgan: Well, it's a global network of computer networks, which allows users to share all sorts of information and computer resources. The system comprises networks interconnected all over the world, from universities and large corporations to commercial online systems and non-profit organizations.

Journalist: And how do you connect yourself up to the Internet? What do you need?

Mr Morgan: Well, you just need a PC, a modem and a telephone line. Not a lot really.

Journalist: And is it easy to install a modem?

Mr Morgan: Oh yes. You just connect one cable of the modem to the communications port of the computer and the other to the telephone line.

Journalist: Right. And I imagine you need special software to get online.

Mr Morgan: Yes, that's right. You need telecommunications software. This enables you to transmit and receive data. To get your Internet identity you have to set up an account with an Internet service provider – a commercial company that offers connection for an annual fee.

Journalist: Do you have to pay a lot of money?

Mr Morgan: Not really. With a standard Internet account you pay just a few pounds. Of course you also have to pay your phone bill for the time connected.

Journalist: Right. And what services are offered by the Internet?

Mr Morgan: It offers services such as e-mail, file transfer, newsgroups, real-time chats and information retrieval on the World Wide Web.

Journalist: The Web is the most important part of the Internet, isn't it? What is the Web?

Mr Morgan: The Web is a huge collection of 'pages' stored on computers all over the world. Web pages contain all sorts of information in the form of text, pictures, sounds and video. They also have links to other resources on the net.

Journalist: OK, right. Thanks very much, Mr Morgan. You've been very helpful.

PHOTOCOPIABLE © Cambridge University Press 2002

3 Reading

A
1 a   2 f   3 e   4 c   5 b   6 g   7 d

B
1 b   2 b   3 a   4 a   5 a

5 A typical web page

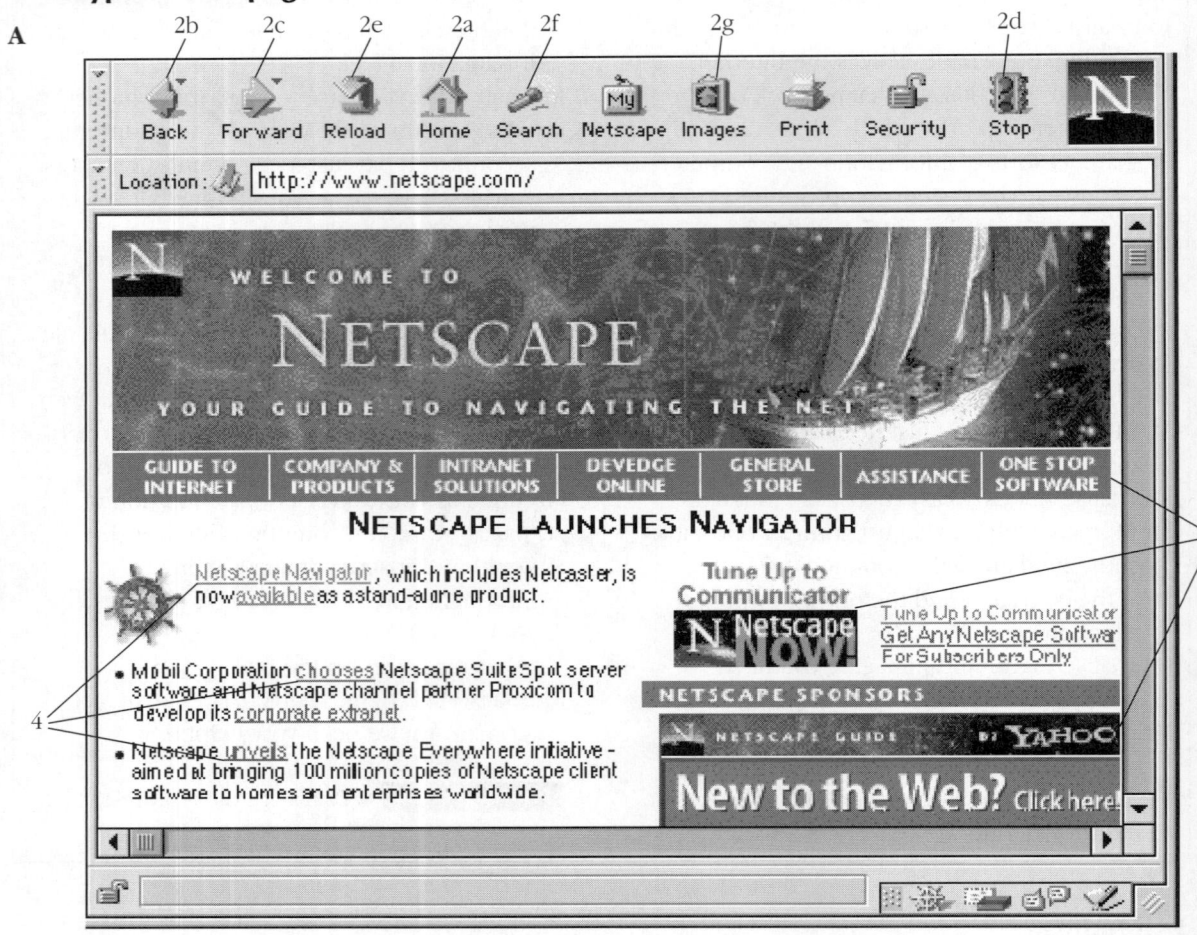

A

[Browser window screenshot showing Netscape toolbar with buttons labeled: Back (2b), Forward (2c), Reload (2e), Home (2a), Search (2f), My Netscape (2g), Images, Print, Security, Stop (2d), and the Netscape page at http://www.netscape.com/]

C

1 http://www.greenpeace.org/
2 http://www.telegraph.co.uk/
3 http://www.ibm.com/
4 http://www.gofly.com/
5 http://www.oscars.org/
6 http://www.yahoo.com/

6 Writing

A

Sender: celia@mail.sendanet.es
Recipient: John Hartley
    <john@ngate.demon.co.uk>
Line that describes the content:
Subject: The Internet and education
An 'attached' file is a document included as part of an e-mail message.

Creative software

Unit		page
19	*Graphics and design*	70
20	*Desktop publishing*	73
21	*Web design*	76
22	*Multimedia*	79

Unit 19 *Graphics and design*

Topics
2-D and 3-D graphics
Tool palette
Transformations

Learning objectives
To identify the function of different graphics tools and to interpret visual representations of them
To acquire basic vocabulary related to graphics packages

Language
Grammar: Gerunds (-*ing* nouns)
Vocabulary: *tool palette, patterns, primitives, attributes, dithering, zoom, rotating, scaling, inverting, rendering,* etc.
Acronyms: *CAD, CAE, CAM*

Skills
Reading: Finding general and specific information to answer questions
Listening: Checking answers to gap-fill passage
Speaking: Describing and completing 2-D and 3-D graphs

Optional materials
A graphics program

Plan

Teacher's activities	Students' activities	Comments
Section page You may want to read through the learning objectives with your students.		
1 Warm-up Pre-teach some vocabulary (e.g. *two-dimensional, three-dimensional*) to prepare SS for the reading passage. (You may like to introduce the lesson by showing SS a graphics program on the computer.)	SS look at the pictures and answer the questions as a whole class.	2-D drawings have no depth – they look flat. 3-D pictures have depth or perspective.
2 Reading Encourage SS to guess the meaning of any new words from the context. Check answers with the whole class.	SS read the passage and answer the questions in pairs.	
3 Listening **A** Give SS a few minutes to complete the passages before playing the cassette. **B** Personalize the activity by asking 'Have you ever used a graphics package with these or similar icons?'	**A** SS read the passage and try to complete it. Then they listen and check their predictions against the cassette. **B** SS match the icons with the definitions.	

4 More about graphics Some of the vocabulary may need to be explained (e.g. *scale, shading*).	**A** SS match the facilities with the definitions. **B** SS label the pictures and compare answers with a partner.	
5 Language work: Gerunds (*-ing* nouns) **A** Highlight in the passage: (i) the functions and uses of gerunds (subject, object, etc.), and (ii) vocabulary related to graphics transformations and rendering.	**A** SS read the passage, identify the gerunds and analyse their function. **B** SS complete the sentences with the gerunds in the box.	SS may confuse *-ing* nouns and *-ing* adjectives. Make sure they understand the difference. Also make sure they understand transforming and rendering techniques.
6 Speaking Check SS understand what they have to do. You may like to write some language input on the board (e.g. the *Useful constructions*). Go round the class and monitor the task.	SS work in pairs, using the information on their relevant page. (They should not look at their partner's page.)	This is a good example of a task which integrates skills.

Evaluation of the unit: ....
....

Answer key

1 Warm-up

1 The car and the business graph are three-dimensional. The map and the plan of the house are two-dimensional. Three-dimensional images represent objects (like the car here) more accurately. In graphs they can also illustrate different quantities more clearly.
2 Cartographers (map makers), car engineers and designers, architects and business executives might use computer graphics.
3 Specialized uses: designers in all kinds of industries to design and test products, engineers (e.g. telephone and electrical engineers) to plan circuits, weather forecasters to show changes in weather, economists to illustrate economic developments, Web designers to create pages for the Internet.

General uses: scientists in research, journalists in broadcasting, teachers.

2 Reading

1 Computer graphics are pictures and drawings produced by the computer.
2 CAD: Computer-Aided Design
  CAE: Computer-Aided Engineering
  CAM: Computer-Aided Manufacturing
3 Computer graphics can be used to develop, model and test car designs before the physical parts are made. This can save money and time.
4 Computer graphics can convey information more effectively, which is a benefit in business.
5 Computer animation is the process of creating objects and pictures which move across the screen.

3 Listening

A

1 package 2 painting 3 graphical
4 circles 5 attributes 6 line 7 icons
8 clicking 9 drawing

B

1 h   9 j
2 h   10 c
3 d   11 l
4 i   12 l
5 f   13 b
6 n   14 g
7 m   15 a
8 k   16 e

4 More about graphics

A

1 e   2 c   3 a   4 f   5 b   6 g   7 d

B

1 scaling 2 rotating 3 inverting
4 slanting 5 black-and-white dithering
6 zoom 7 patterns menu

5 Language work: Gerunds (-ing nouns)

A

line 2	specifying (object of a preposition)
line 4	specifying (object of a preposition)
line 7	moving (object of a verb)
line 7	manipulating (object of a verb)
line 8	translating (object of a preposition)
line 8	rotating (object of a preposition)
line 8	scaling (object of a preposition)
line 9	moving (complement of the subject)
line 11	turning (complement of the subject)
line 12	Scaling (subject of a verb)
line 12	making (complement of the subject)
line 15	rendering (subject of a verb) (Note: The term 'rendering' is an example of 'restrictive apposition', in which the first appositive ('term') is the more general expression.)
line 17	Rendering (subject of a verb)
line 18	shading (object of a verb)

(Note: *corresponding* in line 14 is not a gerund but a present participle, equivalent to an adjectival (relative) clause 'which corresponds'.)

You may like to provide these other examples:

Dithering refers to the technique for making an image seem to have more colours.
Peter is very good at describing scenery.
She is tired of walking.
Today the emphasis is on learning rather than teaching.
Scientists are interested in developing new programming languages.
You can move text by choosing Cut from the Edit menu.

B

1 adding 2 creating 3 processing
4 printing 5 clicking 6 Rendering

6 Speaking

The figures for Graph 1

communications	£3,250
new furniture	£1,800
repairs	£7,880
gas and electricity	£8,500
office supplies	£2,225
books	£2,900
technical equipment	£10,000

The figures for Graph 2

mortgage	£2,875
food	£2,820
entertainment	£1,800
gas and electricity	£1,050
transport	£840
clothes	£1,045
school	£350

Unit 20 *Desktop publishing*

Topics
Desktop publishing
Fonts
Computers for newspapers

Learning objectives
To understand the basic features and vocabulary related to desktop publishing
To write a letter to a newspaper asking for information about the hardware and software used in its production

Language
Grammar: Word formation (affixation, conversion, compounding)

Vocabulary: *DTP package, page layout, imagesetter, service bureaux, font software designer, import,* etc.

Skills
Reading: Checking information
Listening: Understanding specific information
Speaking: Exchanging information about newspapers
Writing: A formal letter requesting information

Optional material
A page-layout program (PageMaker or QuarkXPress)

Plan

Teacher's activities	Students' activities	Comments
1 Warm-up Direct SS' attention to the sample screen, and ask them 'What is desktop publishing?' Elicit some ideas from SS. Then ask them questions 1 and 2. You may like to show them a page-layout program on computer.	SS look at the sample screen, answer the questions and volunteer information about what they know about DTP.	
2 Reading Check answers with the whole class.	**A** SS read to check their answers to Task 1. **B** SS complete the sentences with specific information.	This is designed to help SS understand DTP technologies and applications.
3 Word building Tell SS that affixation and compounding will help them develop their vocabulary. Write the words in the box on the board and add some further examples.	SS can work in pairs.	
4 Listening Before playing the cassette, direct SS' attention to the fonts illustrated here. Emphasize aspects such as style and size.	SS listen to the interview and select the right answers in the multiple-choice exercise.	You may like to give them a photocopy of the transcript. This can help SS understand the contrast between a *scalable font* and a *bit-mapped font*.

Unit 20 *Desktop publishing*

As a follow-up exercise, you could ask SS to identity the fonts used in the Student's Book, so that they get accustomed to identifying font types, sizes and styles.

5 Computers for newspapers
  A Draw SS' attention to the structure of the letter (see Answer key).
     Point out that 'We would be very grateful if you could …' and 'Could you also tell us whether …' are examples of rather formal requests, often used in letters of this kind. You can also advise SS not to use contracted forms in formal letters.
  B Make sure they understand how to exchange the information.
  C This can be set as homework to be done in small groups.

It can be challenging for them to identify fonts, for example: Times Bold at 10 pt. They may like to give their opinion about the typefaces used in the design of the book.

  A SS read the letter and study its format and style.
  B SS exchange information about the hardware and software used by two newspapers.
  C SS can write the letter individually or in small groups.

Evaluation of the unit: ....
....

Answer key

1 Warm-up

Possible answers
1 Texts (from word processors), graphics (from drawing programs), scanned images (from image manipulation programs)
2 Books, newsletters, leaflets, brochures, magazines, newspapers, posters, etc.

2 Reading

B
Possible answers
1 A page layout application can import and combine **text, graphics and scanned images**.
2 Font creation software enables users to **design and create their own fonts**.
3 Imagesetters are used to **print files onto film**.
4 Service bureaux offer services such as **imageset output, laser printer output, scanning equipment**, etc.

3 Word building

1 up<u>grade</u>: affixation; verb
2 im<u>print</u>: affixation; verb
3 <u>print</u>ed: affixation; verb or adjective
4 <u>print</u>-out: compounding; noun
5 inter<u>act</u>ive: affixation; adjective
6 <u>print</u>ing press: compounding; noun
7 pre-<u>press</u>: affixation; noun
8 cre<u>at</u>ive: affixation; adjective
9 ma<u>nipulat</u>ion: affixation; noun
10 <u>publ</u>ishing: affixation; noun or participle
11 <u>publ</u>isher: affixation; noun
12 <u>news</u>letter: compounding; noun
13 <u>vis</u>ually: affixation; adverb
14 <u>type</u>face: compounding; noun
15 pro<u>fess</u>ional: affixation; adjective
16 <u>i</u>magesetter: compounding; noun

> **Tapescript**
>
> Interviewer: Hello, and welcome to this week's edition of *Hotline*. Today we're looking at desktop publishing and here to talk to us is Ros Jackson. Ros is a font software designer and she's going to talk to us a bit about her job. Ros, what exactly is a font – and what is font software?
>
> Ros: Well, a font is a set of characters which all have the same style, shape and size. Font software is software that provides users with a range of fonts. For example, you might have Times Italic in 12 point. 'Times Italic' is the name of the typeface and '12 point' refers to the size.
>
> Interviewer: And who uses this kind of software?
>
> Ros: It's mainly used by people using desktop publishing packages.
>
> Interviewer: And what do they do with all these fonts?
>
> Ros: Well, they choose one that communicates their message in the best way. For promotional leaflets and advertising of any kind, it's important to choose the right font, and we provide them with a good range.
>
> Interviewer: And can you change the fonts in any way once you have them?
>
> Ros: Oh yes, with a font manipulation program you can enlarge scalable fonts, you can stretch them, condense them, rotate them, do all kinds of things with them.
>
> Interviewer: Now you just mentioned 'scalable fonts'. What are these, exactly?
>
> Ros: Well, they are fonts that you can change, as I've just described. You can alter their shape or size because they are stored as an outline and this outline can be changed. They are much more flexible than bit-mapped fonts which can't be changed at all. This kind of font is stored as a whole image made up of dots, not just as an outline, and you get a distorted image of the font if you try to scale it.
>
> Interviewer: And are there different types of scalable fonts produced by different companies?
>
> Ros: Um, there are two main formats, we call them, of scalable fonts: There's TrueType from Apple and Microsoft, and PostScript from Adobe Systems.
>
> Interviewer: And what do you actually do in your job?
>
> Ros: Well, I'm mainly involved in …
>
> **PHOTOCOPIABLE** © Cambridge University Press 2002

4 Listening

See tapescript in panel above.
1 b   2 c   3 b   4 b   5 b

5 Computers for newspapers

A

You may like to draw the students' attention to the following points:
- where you put your address and the address of the person or company you're writing to
- how you write the date
- how you start and end the letter.

75

Unit 21 *Web design*

Topics	Skills
Website design	**Reading:** Finding specific information
Learning objectives	Recognizing basic HTML tags
To understand the basic principles of Web page design	**Listening:** Putting given steps in order
To know and be able to use common modal verbs	**Speaking:** Answering a questionnaire
To acquire the vocabulary related to Web design	**Writing:** Creating basic web pages
Language	**Optional material**
Grammar: Modal verbs	A webpage editor
Vocabulary: *website, homepage, HTML tag, web editor, hyperlink*	**Internet work**
	10 things you can do on the Net

Plan

Teacher's activities	Students' activities	Comments
1 Warm-up Tell SS to examine the webpage illustrated. Elicit answers.	SS look at a typical homepage and try to answer the questions.	
2 Reading Set the task and help SS with new vocabulary. Draw SS' attention to the HTML source code and to the webpage displayed	**A** SS find answers to the questions. **B** Using the text and their intuition, SS try to recognize some basic HTML tags.	SS should understand the basic structure of an HTML document. (See the HELP box in the Answer key.)
3 Language work: modal verbs Go through the HELP box and illustrate the use of modal verbs with more examples, if necessary. Check answers in class feedback.	SS first study the form and semantics of modal verbs. Then they do exercises A and B.	
4 Listening **A** Tell SS to discuss the questions in groups. You may like to write a summary on the board. In **B** and **C**, an expert describes how to design a website. Check answers with the whole class. You may like to give them a copy of the tapescript.	**A** In small groups, SS give examples of good websites they know and discuss what makes a good site. **B** SS listen to the interview and put the steps in the correct order. **C** SS tick (✓) good design principles and cross (✗) the bad ones.	
5 Speaking Check SS' pronunciations and grammar.	In pairs, SS ask and answer the questionnaire.	

6 Creating basic web pages		
A Encourage SS to create their own webpage using a web editor. B You may like to set this as homework.	A SS try and design their homepage. They can use the page in task 2 as a model. B SS find information about their college/company and design a homepage for it.	A and B are like mini-projects. Help SS organise the contents

Evaluation of the unit: ....
....

Answer key

1 Warm-up

Possible answers

1 Companies publish their pages to promote projects and advertise products. Individuals usually create web pages to share information with other users.
2 A **website** is a collection of web **pages**, set up by an organization or an individual, that are usually stored on the same computer. The pages are all linked together. You can move from one page to another by clicking on words and pictures called hyperlinks. Most web sites contain a **home page** which takes you to the other pages. Some sites have a **site map**, which shows the layout of the entire site.
3 a) A home page is the introductory page which tells visitors what information is contained in a Web site. It has links to the other areas of the site. It can also include information such as when a site was built or updated.
   b) A home page is also the default start-up page on which a web browser starts.
4 An Internet portal is a website which offers links to other sites, e-mail, forums, news, etc.

2 Reading

A

1 HTML codes are called tags.
2 They convert text documents into web pages. (They allow you to format the text, add colour, insert images and links, etc.)
3 A web editor.
4 By clicking the option 'Page source' in the browser's menu. (*Note*: this option depends on the web browser)
5 Web pages on a site are linked together through a system of hyperlinks.

> HELP
> *This is the structure of a basic HTML document:*
> <HTML>
> <HEAD>
> <TITLE> My web page </TITLE>
> </HEAD>
> <BODY> The text on my page goes here </BODY>
> </HTML>

B

1 b   2 e   3 g   4 f   5 c   6 i
7 j   8 a   9 h   10 d

3 Language work: Modal Verbs

A

can, may, should

B

1 must   2 could   3 can   4 must
5 might   6 can't   7 May   8 should

4 Listening

B

See tapescript in panel.
1 Decide the content and structure for the website
2 Write and format the text
3 Insert computer graphics and sounds

Unit 21 Web design

Tapescript

Interviewer: Good morning. In the studio with me is Sarah Almy, a web designer from Media Express. Sarah, what should we do before we start building a website?

Sarah: First of all, you should plan it carefully. You have to decide what sort of information you're going to include and how you are going to organize the contents. You should also plan a home page; this is the starting point of your website, like the table of contents of a book. So it's a good idea to design the website on paper first. Making a few diagrams will help you divide the contents and clarify the relationships between the documents.

Interviewer: That sounds sensible. What editing tool do you recommend?

Sarah: I recommend using a web editor; it will make it easier to create your pages. You can download a web editor from the Internet.

Interviewer: Right. I suppose a big part of the job is writing the text and formatting the webpages.

Sarah: Yes. You need to type the text and decide the formatting effects. You can apply styles to text to add emphasis or to make it more appealing to your readers.

Interviewer: OK. What about graphics and sounds?

Sarah: Well, that's the next step. You can insert all sorts of computer images and sounds. But they should have a clear purpose, some sort of communicative intention. Don't insert photos or animations just to make the pages look nice; and avoid placing a large number of graphics on your pages.

Interviewer: Why's that?

Sarah: Because graphics can take a long time to download and visitors give up if the pages take too long to appear.

Interviewer: I see. Any advice about the use of colour?

Sarah: It's fun to experiment with colour. You may like to choose different colours for the background and the text. But make sure that all the text is easy to read and don't use very bright colours.

Interviewer: OK. What's next?

Sarah: Once you've created and saved a few pages, it's time to join them together with hyperlinks. A good design principle is not to put too many links on one page, people may lose patience or get distracted. And check that all the links on your web pages are correct since web addresses sometimes change.

Interviewer: So, careful with the links. What shall I do if I decide to publish my web pages on the Internet?

Sarah: OK. To publish your web pages, you have to find a web server and then transfer all the files from your PC to the server. This is called 'going live'. But, before that, you should open the pages in your browser to see how they will look online. This will allow you to check that all the links work and view any animation on your pages in action.

Interviewer: Right. Any final comment?

Sarah: Yes, try to keep the pages updated, improve the content and design if necessary. And the final touch: include the date to show that your site is up-to-date.

Interviewer: Thank you very much.

PHOTOCOPIABLE © Cambridge University Press 2002

4 Weave together related pages with hyperlinks.
5 Publish the website
6 Keep website updated.

C
1 Right   2 Right   3 Wrong   4 Wrong
5 Wrong   6 Wrong   7 Right   8 Right

Unit 22 *Multimedia*

Topic
Multimedia technology

Learning objectives
To understand the main components and applications of multimedia systems
To acquire the basic terminology related to multimedia technology

Language
Grammar: First and second conditional clauses
Vocabulary: *multimedia PC, stereo speaker, sound card, MIDI, animation, encyclopedia, streaming, webcast, clips, video editing*

Multimedia file formats on the Web: *.htm, .gif, .jpg, .wav, .ra, .avi, .mpg, .zip,* etc.

Skills
Listening: Completing a diagram from information in a conversation
Identifying different types of software
Reading: Matching headings with texts
Finding specific information
Writing: Describing the process of making a movie on a PC.

Internet work
MP3 music

Plan

Teacher's activities	Students' activities	Comments
1 Multimedia is here! Elicit from SS the elements integrated in multimedia presentations. Write them on the board.	Using the picture and their own knowledge, SS share their ideas about the sources and components of multimedia applications.	
2 Listening **A** Direct SS' attention to the diagram. Check answers with the whole class. **B** Play the audio material again and check answers. After the task, ask SS to describe the components of a multimedia PC at home / school / work.	**A** SS listen and complete the diagram. **B** SS listen again and try to answer the questions individually. Then they compare answers with a partner.	When talking about multimedia, SS should be able to distinguish between hardware components and software sources.
3 Reading You may need to explain some of the vocabulary. Give SS an opportunity to compare answers with a partner before going through the answers with the whole class.	SS read the headings at **A** before reading the passage. For **B** and **C**, SS should look back at the text and find passages to support their answers.	Make sure SS understand key words like *hypertext*, *MIDI, streaming technique, video editing.*
4 Language work: *If*-clauses The study of conditional clauses is contextualized by using examples connected with the theme of the unit. You may like to present first and second conditionals on the board. Check answers with the whole class.	SS first try to do the language work individually.	For weaker SS a contrastive analysis of conditional clauses with their own language may be helpful.

Unit 22 Multimedia

5 Multimedia on the Web You may like to explain the term 'plug-ins', the small programs that help us manage different multimedia elements.	SS read through the text and find specific information.	
6 Writing Draw SS attention to the pictures describing the process. Help them with vocabulary and grammar.	Using the pictures, SS describe the process of making a movie on a PC.	
7 Listening You may want to play the cassette twice.	SS listen to the descriptions and number the items in the correct order.	The aim of this task is to recycle different types of software covered in the preceding units.

Evaluation of the unit: ....
....

Answer key

1 Multimedia is here!

Possible answers

Text, graphics, scanned images, photographs, animated images, sound (music, voice annotations), and video sequences, in any combination.

2 Listening

See tapescript in panel on page 81 and the answer key below.

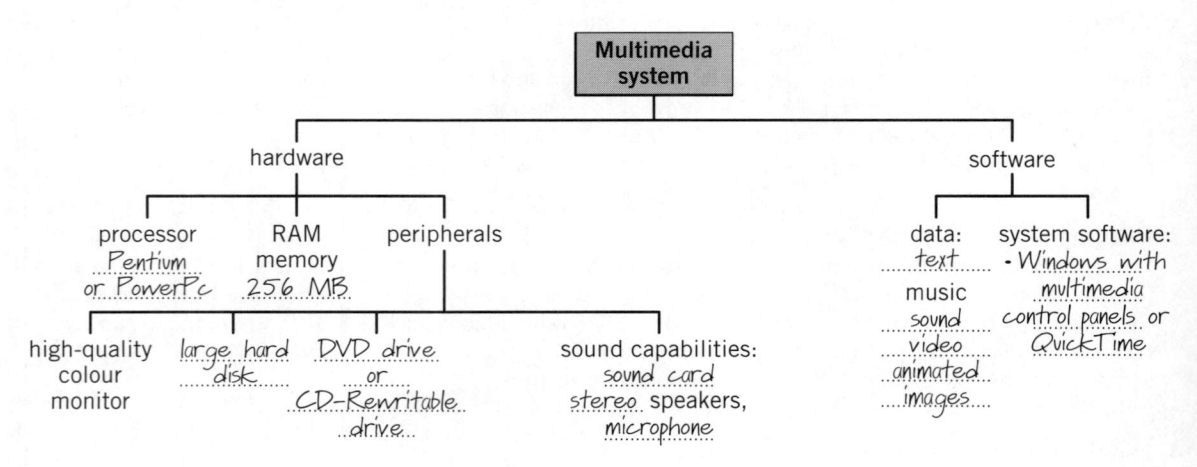

```
                        Multimedia
                          system
              ┌──────────────┴──────────────┐
           hardware                      software
     ┌────────┼────────┐              ┌──────┴──────┐
  processor  RAM    peripherals     data:      system software:
  Pentium   memory                  text       - Windows with
  or PowerPc 256 MB                 music         multimedia
                                    sound        control panels or
                                    video        QuickTime
                                    animated
                                    images
```

high-quality colour monitor | large hard disk | DVD drive or CD-Rewritable drive | sound capabilities: sound card, stereo speakers, microphone

80

> **Tapescript**
>
> Customer: This is an obvious question, but what exactly is 'multimedia'?
>
> Sales assistant: Well, 'multimedia' refers to the technologies and applications that integrate sound, music, video, text, images, animation and any other media in any other combination.
>
> Customer: And why would you want to have it? What are its advantages over traditional computing?
>
> Sales assistant: Well, it's just very interesting and entertaining to use. A lot of people really enjoy using a program with sound and motion pictures. It's much more fun than an ordinary program, and much more fun than watching TV or a video because you can interact with it – you can choose what you want to watch, listen to or write. Watching TV is just very passive, whereas with multimedia you can actually do things so that you get much more involved.
>
> Customer: OK. And what's the basic hardware you need to run an application?
>
> Sales assistant: Well, they say you really need a Pentium or PowerPC, with at least 256 megabytes of RAM. You'd also need a high quality colour monitor, plenty of storage capacity on your hard disk and a DVD drive.
>
> As an alternative to the DVD, you can have a CD-Rewritable drive.
>
> Customer: I suppose you also need some sort of sound capablilities.
>
> Sales assistant: Yes, of course. Modern PCs come with a sound card, stereo speakers and a microphone.
>
> Customer: Right. And what about software? Is there a standard operating system for multimedia work?
>
> Sales assistant: No, not yet. Microsoft has Windows with multimedia control panels to work with audio and video files. Apple has Quicktime, a system extension that you use to create and run your own animation and video sequences. Quicktime can also run on Windows.
>
> Customer: And can you make your own movies on computer?
>
> Sales assistant: Yes, but you need special software and …(fade)
>
> **PHOTOCOPIABLE** © Cambridge University Press 2002

B

1 Multimedia is the integration of text, sound, graphics, animation and movies on the computer screen.
   (Note: Multimedia is also defined as the integration of the existing technologies of audio, video, animation and telecommunications with traditional computing.)
2 Multimedia computers add the crucial element of 'interaction'. In a TV presentation the viewer is just a passive observer of sights and sounds.
3 QuickTime.

3 Reading

A

1 The potential of using multimedia
2 Sound, Music, MIDI
3 Editing photos and making movies in a few minutes.
4 CDs and DVDs full of pictures, action and sound!

B
Suggested answers

1 Multimedia PCs can integrate text with graphics and video.
2 You need to have a sound board on your PC to hear speech and music.
3 Most multimedia software is distributed on optical disks (CD-ROMs or DVDs).
4 Digital cameras store photos in a memory chip.
5 There are language courses available on CD-ROM.

C
1 c   2 b   3 a   4 e   5 d

4 Language work: *If*-clauses

A

1 If you **upgrade** your PC, you**'ll be able** to run multimedia applications.
present simple + future (*will* + verb) = *If*-clause Type I (possible situation)

2 If the marketing manager **had** a multimedia system, she **could make** more effective presentations.
past simple + conditional tense (*would* + verb) = *If*-clause Type II (unlikely, or imaginary situation)

B

1 get
2 had
3 don't have
4 came
5 would buy

5 Multimedia on the Web

A

1 The extension added to a file name describes the file's contents and helps us identify the format.
2 html: Hypertext Markup Language
3 .gif
4 RealPlayer
5 .avi, .mov and .mpg (or .mpeg)
6 .mpg (or .mpeg)
7 .zip

7 Listening

See tapescript in panel.

1 Educational software
2 Graphics and design
3 Database program
4 Multimedia application
5 Web editor
6 Musical software
7 DTP

Tapescript

1 This application helps students identify the stars in the night sky. It also includes a series of demonstrations of the laws of physics.
2 This is a basic drawing program with which you can develop graphics for a variety of uses including business graphs, architectural renderings and engineering drawings.
3 This package allows you to store, manipulate and retrieve data. Information is entered on the program via fields. With the relevant information, you can keep track of stock, sales, orders, invoices, clients' addresses and other details.
4 This is one of the best authoring programs on the market. QuickMedia allows you to combine text, graphics, speech, animation, scanned images and full-motion video from Windows and Macintosh applications.
5 This program enables you to create web pages without writing HTML commands. You can easily include frames, image maps, multimedia elements and interactive effects in your page designs.
6 This program includes samples of sounds and a wide range of functions – scales, intervals, melody and rhythm. It's fully MIDI compatible. Easy to use and fun.
7 This is a page-layout program with many powerful features and typographical precision. It allows text and graphics to flow automatically from one page to the next.

PHOTOCOPIABLE © Cambridge University Press 2002

Programming

Unit		page
23	*Program design*	84
24	*Languages*	87
25	*The Java revolution*	91
26	*Jobs in computing*	94

Unit 23 *Program design*

Topics
Programming

Learning objectives
To understand basic concepts in programming, and acquire vocabulary connected with it

Language
Grammar: Infinitive constructions

Vocabulary: *algorithm, flowchart, coding, machine code, bug, debug, assembly languages, source program, object program, compiler,* etc.
Prefixes and suffixes

Skills
Reading: Finding answers to questions about the main features of programming languages
Listening: Putting given steps in order

Plan

Teacher's activities	Students' activities	Comments
Section page You may want to look at the learning objectives with your students. **1 Warm-up** A Elicit ideas from SS.	 A SS brainstorm their ideas about programming. B SS complete the definitions of technical terms and practise their pronunciation.	 B This activity is designed to pre-teach some of the new words in the unit.
2 Listening *Option:* Ask SS to say 'stop' or raise a hand after each programming step.	A SS listen and arrange the steps in the correct order. B SS take notes and explain each step in their own words.	
3 Reading Ask SS to provide evidence from the text for their answers. Make sure they understand basic concepts (e.g. *high-level language, compiler, machine code*).	Alone or in pairs, SS read the text to find answers to the questions.	Some SS may find it difficult to understand technical terms associated with programming. Encourage them to use the Glossary.
4 Word building A You could remind SS of the adjectival and nominal suffixes they saw in Unit 7 before introducing the task. B Elicit as many verbs as you can, including ones that do not actually exist! It is a good way of encouraging SS to experiment with language.	A SS decide what part of speech the words are and complete the sentences with the correct form. B SS work out what the verbs with and without *de-* mean in their own language. Then they think of other verbs in English beginning with *de-*.	

| 5 Language work: Infinitive constructions
Read through the examples with SS before setting **A** to **C**. Check answers with the whole class. | Alone or in pairs, SS do the activities. | **C** This may be difficult for some SS. Explain how specific verbs are followed by either the *-ing* form or the infinitive. |

Evaluation of the unit: ....
....

Answer key

1 Warm-up

B
1 a given problem
2 the various parts of the program
3 language
4 binary numbers
5 may occur in programs

2 Listening

See tapescript in panel.
1 Understand the problem and plan the solution.
2 Make a flowchart of the program.
3 Write the instructions in coded form and compile the program.
4 Test and correct the program.
5 Provide documentation of the program.

3 Reading

1 No, computers don't understand human languages because the central processor operates only on binary code numbers (machine code, 1s and 0s).
2 In a low-level language, each instruction is equivalent to a single machine code instruction. However, in a high-level language, each statement is generally translated into many machine code instructions.
3 An assembler is a special program which converts a program written in a low-level language into machine code.

Tapescript
First of all, you have to understand exactly what the problem is, and define it clearly. This means you have to decide in a general way how to solve the problem.

The next step is to design an algorithm, which is a step-by-step plan of instructions used to solve the problem. You do this in a flowchart. You use special symbols to show how the computer works through your program – where it makes decisions, where it starts and ends, and things like that.

Then you translate the steps in the flowchart into instructions written in a computer language. You usually write these in a high-level language like BASIC or Pascal. You have to then use something called a compiler which translates the instructions into machine code, which is the only language understood by the processor.

Once you've written your program you have to test it with sample data to see if there are any bugs or errors. Usually there are, so the program has to be cleared of them or 'debugged'.

And then last of all you have to write instructions explaining to people how to use it. A great program is not much use unless people know how to use it.

PHOTOCOPIABLE © Cambridge University Press 2002

4 The function of compilers is to convert a source program into an object program. Compilers convert a program written in a high-level language into a program written in a lower level language.
5 A 'source program' is written in a language that cannot be directly processed by the computer but requires compilation into an 'object program'.
6 In the future, computers may be able to understand natural languages thanks to Artificial Intelligence.

4 Word building

compile (verb)   compiler (noun)
compilation (noun)
1 compilation   2 compiler   3 compile

program (noun)   programmer (noun)
programming (noun)   programmable (adjective)
4 programmers   5 program
6 programming

bug (noun)   debug (verb)
debugger (noun)   debugging (noun)
7 debugging   8 bug   9 debugger

B
defrost (frost), debrief (brief), declassify (classify), decode (code), decompose (compose), decentralize (centralize)
(Note: Other verbs you could suggest are: *decompress, deconstruct, decontaminate, dehumanize, dehydrate, depersonalize, destabilize*. Point out that many common verbs in English which begin with *de-* cannot be divided into prefix and base form in this way, e.g. *decide, deliver, demand, depart*.)

5 Language work: Infinitive constructions

A
1 It is advisable to test the program under different conditions.
2 It is expensive to set up a data-processing area.
3 It is unusual for a program to work correctly the first time it is tested.
4 It is difficult for students to learn FORTRAN.
5 It is important to consider the capabilities of the programming language.
6 It is quite easy to write instructions in BASIC.

B
line 1:   cannot understand
line 3:   can understand
line 11:   can be translated
line 40:   can be made
line 41:   will be
line 43:   may be able

C
1 a I remember shutting down the computer before I left the room. (I shut down the computer, and now I remember it.)
  We *remember doing* things in the past – things that we did.
  b Please remember to buy the new program. (Don't forget to buy the new program.)
  We *remember to do* things that we have to do.
2 a They stopped to look at the flowchart. (They paused, in the middle of something else, in order to look at the flowchart.)
  b They stopped looking at the flowchart. (They didn't look at the flowchart any more.)
3 a I like studying C. (I 'enjoy' studying C).
  b I like to study C in the evenings. (It does not imply 'enjoyment', but a habit or choice.)
4 a It has started to rain.
  b It has started raining. (With verbs like *begin* and *start* we can use either the *-ing* form or the infinitive without much difference in meaning.)
5 a He needs to work harder. (It's necessary for him to work harder.)
  b This hard disk needs repairing. (This hard disk needs to be repaired.)
  After *need*, an *-ing* form has a passive meaning.

Unit 24 *Languages*

<table>
<tr><td>

Topic
Computer languages: VoiceXML, Visual BASIC, C

Learning objectives
To ask and answer questions about computer languages
To understand short descriptions of specific languages
To recognize acronyms and abbreviations related to computer languages

Language
Grammar: The passive

</td><td>

Vocabulary: *BASIC, COBOL, LOGO, Pascal, SQL, VoiceXML, Voice portal*

Skills
Reading: Finding specific information
Listening: Selecting the most relevant information to complete a table
Speaking: Asking and answering questions to complete a table
Writing: A paragraph describing C

</td></tr>
</table>

Plan

Teacher's activities	*Students' activities*	*Comments*
1 Warm-up Write SS' list of languages on the board.	SS make a list of languages individually; then brainstorm their ideas with the teacher.	
2 The VoiceXML language Ask SS to look carefully at the table, then ask them the questions.	SS study the table and find answers to the questions.	VoiceXML is a new computer language that makes web content accessible via voice and telephone.
3 Language work: The passive Provide more examples illustrating passive tenses and forms, if necessary. Check answers with the whole class.	Alone or in pairs, SS complete the sentences with the correct passive forms.	
4 Speaking This information-gap task focuses on speaking, but also involves reading, listening and writing. Tell SS to ask and answer questions as in the example.	SS should not look at each other's information. They complete their tables by asking their partner questions.	
5 A short description of Visual BASIC Check answers with the whole class.	SS put the verbs in brackets in a suitable tense form. They work individually.	As well as providing factual information, the passage gives practice in verb tenses, forms and voices.

6 Listening

A You may like to write the table on the board.
B Monitor the writing of the paragraph. Check structures and vocabulary.

A SS listen to the conversation and complete the table.
B Using the information in the table and in the listening passage, SS write a short description of C.

C is a leading programming language. The illustration shows a simple C program.

Evaluation of the unit: ....
....

Answer key

1 Warm-up

Possible list of computer languages
BASIC, COBOL, FORTRAN, Pascal, C, LOGO, LISP, PROLOG, ADA language, FORTH, Java, HTML, XML, VoiceXML, etc.

2

The VoiceXML language
1 VMXL means Voice Extensible Markup Language.
2 VoiceXML was created by a working group of four companies – AT&T, Lucent, Motorola and IBM.
3 It was developed in 2000.
4 For input, it uses voice recognition. For output it uses recorded audio content and a speech synthesis system (which converts text into spoken words).
5 VoiceXML gives you access to the Internet by using your voice. The most suitable applications are: voice web portals, voice-equipped intranets, e-commerce and home devices controlled by voice.
6 The voice web can be more convenient than the graphical, visual Web when we want to obtain information quickly about sports, weather, news etc. Banks can use VoiceXML to deliver account balances and share prices to their clients. Speech recognition can also be used to conduct business over the Web. You don't need to have a PC with a keyboard and a mouse. You just need a telephone to access the Internet content.

3 Language work: The passive

1 is used
2 are written
3 must be translated
4 was developed
5 were designed
6 has (just) been released
7 will be programmed

4 Speaking

Computer language	Date	Characteristics	Uses
COBOL (**Co**mmon **B**usiness **O**riented **L**anguage)	1958–59	Easy to read. Able to handle very large files. Written in English.	Mainly used for business applications.
Visual BASIC (**B**eginner's **A**ll-purpose **S**ymbolic **I**nstruction **C**ode)	1964–65	High-level programming language. Interactive. Easy to learn. Displays error messages that help users to correct mistakes. Has a large number of dialects.	General purpose language. Used to teach programming.

Pascal (named after the famous scientist Blaise Pascal)	1970–73	Structured language with algorithmic features designed for fast execution of the object program. A fast compiler called TurboPascal was created in 1982 – very popular.	General purpose. Often used in colleges and universities to teach programming.
LOGO	1969	Easy to learn. Flexible – it can do maths, make lists, construct graphs, etc. Its drawing capabilities allow children to construct simple graphics programs.	Designed for use in schools to encourage children to experiment with programming.
SQL (**S**tructured **Q**uery **L**anguage) Introduced by Oracle Corp.	1979	Supports distributed databases, which run on several different computer systems. Allows various users on a LAN to access the same database at the same time.	A standard query language used for requesting information from a database. It allows users to specify search criteria in databases.

5 A short description of Visual BASIC

1 developed   2 is used   3 stands
4 was created   5 writing   6 add
7 be chosen   8 takes   9 drag
10 enables

6 Listening

See tapescript in panel on page 90.

A

Developed by	Date	Characteristics	Uses	Extensions
Dennis Ritchie at **Bell Laboratories**.	**1972**	Created to replace **a language called 'B'**. The language is small, **efficient and portable.**	Originally designed for **UNIX operating systems.** Today it is used to **write system software and commercial applications programs**.	C++ and **Objective C**. Object-oriented languages.

Unit 24 *Languages*

Tapescript

Vicky: Today we're going to look at the programming language C. This was originally designed for UNIX operating systems. Does anyone know who developed it?

Student 1: Wasn't it Bell?

Vicky: Yes, that's right – it was developed by a man called Dennis Ritchie at Bell Laboratories in the States in 1972.

Student 2: Why is it called 'C'?

Vicky: Does anyone know? No? Well, it was called 'C' because it replaced the language used to produce the original version of UNIX which was called 'B'.

Student 2: Was there an 'A' language?

Vicky: I don't think so! C is very popular today because it's small, so it's not too hard to learn, it's very efficient and it's portable so you can use it with all kinds of computers. A lot of software engineers use C to write system software and commercial applications programs for mini, micro and personal computers. There are also new versions of C – there's C++ and Objective C. These extensions incorporate the power of object-oriented programming. Does anyone know anything about object-oriented programming?

Student 3: Isn't it a new type of programming that centres on the thing you're working on – a piece of text, or a bit of graphics or a table?

Vicky: Yes, that's right. In the past, programmers had to write complex programs which covered everything you could do to text and graphics. With object-oriented programming, however, the programmer concentrates on particular things, and gives each object specific functions which can be altered without changing the entire program. For example, an object-oriented word processing program treats bits of data as 'objects', whether they are tables, pieces of text or graphics. The objects themselves include operations to allow you to display them or print them. To add a new graphics format the programmer needs to rework just the graphics object; the main program remains untouched. What's the advantage of this kind of program do you think?

Student 1: It's quicker to use?

Vicky: Yes, that's right. Now let's have a look at a small program written in C …

PHOTOCOPIABLE © Cambridge University Press 2002

B

Possible answer

C is a high-level programming language developed by Dennis Ritchie at Bell Laboratories in 1972. It was originally designed for UNIX operating systems. Today it is also used to write commercial applications programs. This portable language is small and very efficient. There are various object-oriented extensions to C such as C++ and Objective C, which represent a new style of programming.

Unit 25 — *The Java revolution*

Topic
The Java language

Learning objectives
To learn basic vocabulary associated with the Java language
To be able to talk about personal experience of using computers.

Language
Grammar: The past simple: regular and irregular verbs.
The different pronunciations of the suffix -ed.
Vocabulary: *Java applet, plug-in, bytecode, interpreter, multi-threaded, download*
Common computing terms

Skills
Reading: Understanding the basic features of Java
Listening: Checking answers to a gap-fill exercise
Speaking: Asking and answering questions about personal experience of computers
Telling the class about a partner's experience of computers
Writing: Writing about your experience of computers

Optional materials
The Java website at http://java.sun.com

Plan

Teacher's activities	Students' activities	Comments
1 Warm-up **A** Go through the task and elicit answers to the question 'What exactly is Java?' Direct SS' attention to the pictures and captions illustrating Java applets, and ask the questions. **B** Let them use the Glossary.	**A** SS look at the illustrations and answer the questions about Java. **B** SS guess the meaning of key words that appear in Task 2.	Some SS may have heard or used the Java language.
2 Reading Write any useful vocabulary on the board. In class feedback, ask SS to provide evidence from the text to support their answers.	SS read the statements and the passage and make changes to the false statements. Then, in pairs, they discuss their answers.	
3 Vocabulary These exercises revise phrases or terms that are frequently found together.	In **A** and **B**, SS match each word on the left with its partner on the right to make common computing terms.	
4 Language work: The past simple **A** This part is designed to help students recognize and practise the pronunciation of the suffix -ed. First, direct their attention to the grammar box. Then set the task.	**A** SS listen to the verbs on the cassette and put them in the right column.	Some SS may have trouble deciding whether a past tense verb is pronounced /t/ or /d/. SS can also overgeneralize the pronunciation /ɪd/.

Unit 25 *The Java revolution*

B This passage includes background information about the Java language. It recycles regular and irregular past tenses.	B SS fill in the missing verbs in the correct tense. They then listen to the cassette and check their answers.	Make sure they pronounce /ɪd/ only after the sounds /t/ or /d/.
5 Your experience with computers A Go round and check SS' use of tenses. B Circulate and prompt further questions where necessary. C Choose a few SS to tell the class briefly about their partners. Ask a few questions to get an idea of the average 'computer history'.	A SS write sentences about the different stages in their 'computer history'. B SS share their experiences with another student. C SS tell the class about their partner's experience.	A Though not directly related to the theme of the unit, this task provides a good opportunity to practise the language of Task 4.

Evaluation of the unit: ....
....

Answer key

1 Warm-up

A

1 Help:
Java is a high level programming language developed by Sun in 1995. It's specially designed to run on the Web. Small Java programs are called applets and can be downloaded automatically on web pages. Java can run on any computer.
The Java technology is not only a programming language; it is also a computing platform, including Java workstations, the JavaOS and stand-alone applications.
2 Some students may be familiar with Java applets on the web. For example, they let you watch animations and play interactive games.

2 Reading

1 Java was invented by <u>Sun Microsystems</u>.
2 Small applications written in Java are called '<u>applets</u>'.
3 With the <u>compiler</u>, a program is first converted into Java bytecodes.
4 Java is compatible with most computing platforms.
5 The Java language is <u>multi-threaded</u>, <u>various parts executing at the same time</u>.
6 Java <u>lets</u> you watch animated characters on your webpages.
7 ActiveX and Shockwave <u>are competitors</u> for Java.

3 Vocabulary

A
1 b   2 a   3 g   4 f   5 c
6 d   7 e

B
1 c   2 f   3 d   4 a   5 b   6 e

4 Language work: The past simple

A

/t/	/d/	/ɪd/
developed	described	decided
asked	supplied	generated
produced	programmed	persuaded
watched	combined	interpreted
published	scaled	
	arranged	

B
(1) decided
(2) developed
(3) called
(4) had
(5) based
(6) renamed
(7) could
(8) were
(9) began
(10) supported

Unit 26 — *Jobs in computing*

Topics
Jobs such as programmers, DTP operators, computer operators

Learning objectives
To discuss personal qualities and professional skills needed for computing
To write a letter applying for a job

Language
Grammar: The past simple and the present perfect
For, since, ago
Vocabulary: Word field: personal qualities and professional skills (adjectives and nouns)

Jobs: *programmer, DTP operator, computer operator*, etc.

Skills
Reading: Identifying the qualities and skills required for jobs from advertisements
Speaking: Discussing qualities and abilities required for particular jobs
Listening: Taking notes about a candidate from a job interview
Writing: Letter of application for a specific job

Internet work
The job of your dreams?

Plan

Teacher's activities	Students' activities	Comments
1 Reading A Explain abbreviations if necessary: *CV* = curriculum vitae *DTP* = desktop publishing. Encourage SS to help each other with new vocabulary. B Ask individual SS if they would be interested in any of the jobs. C Ask SS to justify their answer.	A SS read the two advertisements and, in pairs, decide which qualities are necessary or desirable for the jobs. B SS answer the question orally. C SS look carefully at the personal profile of Charles Graham, choose the most appropriate job for him, and give reasons.	
2 Language work: Past activities A Provide some other examples with *for, since* and *ago* if you need to. B Introduce the letter by explaining that it was written by an applicant for the job of Senior Programmer advertised in Task 1. Check answers with the whole class.	A SS complete the sentences with *for, since* or *ago*. Then they explain the difference in meaning between the two sentences. B SS complete the letter with the correct verb tenses and forms.	This is an opportunity to discuss the contrast between the present perfect and past simple.
3 Listening Explain to SS that they're going to hear Chris Scott from Digitum interviewing Sarah Brown. They need to complete his notes about Ms Brown.		

You may need to play the recording two or three times. Check answers with the whole class. **4 Writing** Read through the advert and notes with SS and help them relate the notes to the job. You may want to discuss with them how they are going to organize their ideas in paragraphs, and to remind them of the layout of a formal letter. Go round the class as they write, checking that they are using past simple and present perfect tenses correctly. (You may like to set this task for homework.)	SS listen and complete the notes. They compare answers in pairs. SS read the advert and identify what the company is looking for. They then read the notes about María and see what aspects of her experience are relevant. SS can use the letter in Task 2 as a model.	

Evaluation of the unit: ....
....

Answer key

1 Reading

A

Some other qualities or abilities which could be added to the list:

enthusiasm   good communication skills
accuracy   creativity
reliability versatility
confidence   ability to work under pressure
punctuality ability to cope with routine work

C
Possible answers
Taking into account Charles Graham's experience and qualifications, the most suitable job for him is the post of DTP operator.

2 Language work: Past activities

A
1 since   2 for   3 for   4 ago   5 since
a 'I've worked for a year as a senior programmer' means 'I started to work as a senior programmer and I am still working'.

b 'I worked for a year as a senior programmer' means 'I was a senior programmer once but I am not any longer'.

B
1 apply   2 was advertised
3 have worked/have been working
4 worked   5 have (now) been   6 have won
7 spent   8 made

3 Listening

A
See tapescript in panel on page 96.
Qualifications:
- University: **Computer Sciences degree from Aston University**

Work experience:
- At NCR **worked as analyst programmer for a year**
- What was software used for? **General commercial use**

Tapescript

Mr Scott: I see you did a computer sciences degree at Aston University and you spent your sandwich year with British Gas. How was that?

Ms Brown: It was great. I really enjoyed it. It was really good to get some work experience and apply some of the ideas I'd learnt at college.

Mr Scott: And then you went to NCR. What did you do there?

Ms Brown: I worked as an analyst programmer for a year. I wrote software for general commercial use. The programs were for use on IBM mainframes and minicomputers.

Mr Scott: Right. And have you worked with databases at all?

Ms Brown: Yes, quite a bit. I usually work with Microsoft Access and dBase 5.

Mr Scott: Good. And what about your present job? What do you do at Intelligent Software?

Ms Brown: Well, I write programs in COBOL for use in large retail chains. I write instructions, test the programs and prepare the documentation.

Mr Scott: Fine. That sounds the sort of experience we're looking for. What about foreign languages? Do you have any?

Ms Brown: Yes. I can speak Italian and a bit of Spanish. I've been studying Spanish for the past eight months.

Mr Scott: Good. Well, your current job sounds quite interesting. Why do you want to leave it?

Ms Brown: Well, I've been there for two years and I want something more demanding. I'd like more responsibility and I'd like to learn about a new industry.

PHOTOCOPIABLE © Cambridge University Press 2002

- What computers were used? **IBM mainframes and minicomputers**
- Knowledge of databases? **Microsoft Access and dBase 5**

Reasons for applying: **wants something more demanding and more responsibility and wants to learn about a new industry**

Computers tomorrow

Unit		page
27	*Electronic communications*	98
28	*Internet issues*	101
29	*LANS and WANS*	104
30	*New technologies*	108

Unit 27 *Electronic communications*

Topic
Data communications systems
Cybercafés

Learning objectives
To talk about different data communication systems
To understand how electronic communications work
To acquire specific vocabulary related to telecommunications

Language
Vocabulary: *Fax, bulletin board system, modem, kilobits per second, teletext, commercial online service, download, sysop, cybercafé, ADSL, etc.*

Prefixes: *tele-, auto-, trans-, inter-*

Skills
Reading: Understanding general and specific information about telecommunications
Listening: Listening to find out if the statements are true or false
Speaking: Planning a cybercafé with a partner
Writing: Writing a mini-project

Optional materials
A fax machine, a modem, photos of a cybercafé

Internet work
What is Internet 2?

Plan

Teacher's activities	Students' activities	Comments
Section page You may want to point out the learning objectives to the SS.		
1 Before you read Write the data communications services suggested by SS on the board.	SS brainstorm ideas about the questions.	
2 Reading A Direct SS' attention to the illustrations and captions. Clarify the function of a modem, if necessary. Optional activity: Ask SS if they themselves use any of these methods of communication and, if so, to explain their advantages. B Comprehension puzzle. Check answers with the whole class.	A SS decide which data transmission system is most appropriate for certain requirements. Then they read the text and check their answers. B SS complete the sentences and write the words in the puzzle. C SS link the pairs of words that mean the same.	SS may have some problems with specific vocabulary: *BBS, download, upload, shareware,* etc. Let them use the Glossary and make sure they understand the difference between *Internet service providers* and *commercial online services*. **C** is a review of telecommunications vocabulary.
3 Word building A Remind SS that recognizing the part of speech of a word can help them understand its meaning. B Check SS understand the meaning of the prefixes *auto-, trans-, inter-*. Write the words they suggest on the board.	A SS look at the list of words and decide what part of speech each one is, and where the main stress falls. B SS build up new words by using the prefixes. They can use dictionaries.	

4 Listening

A This is a warm-up activity to get SS ready for listening. Ask SS if they have ever been to an Internet café and, if so, to explain their experience.

B After listening, you may like to give SS a photocopy of the interview.

C Read through the task and HELP box. Encourage SS to design their own cybercafé. Suggest visiting a cybercafé if there is one in town. You may like to set this mini-project for homework.

A SS answer the questions orally.

B SS listen to the interview and say whether the statements are true or false.

C SS can do the project in pairs or small groups.

Answer key

1 Before you read

1 One PC can be connected to another in the same building by using circuits over a network. If the computers are further away from each other, they can be linked by adding modems and connecting them to the telephone line.

2 Data communication systems:
- a computer network (computer devices are interconnected to allow users to exchange files, and share hardware resources)
- fax services
- telex (a system of communication using teleprinters)
- teletext (a system of communicating information by using television signals)
- the Internet (allows anyone with a PC, a modem and a telephone to have access to a wide range of information services: *e-mail, mailing lists, the Web, newsgroups, chats, FTP, Telnet*, etc.)
- local bulletin board systems (BBS).

2 Reading

A
Suggested answers
1 b   2 a   3 e   4 d   5 c

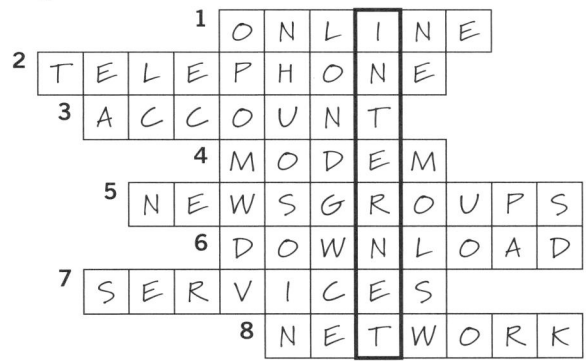

B
1. ONLINE
2. TELEPHONE
3. ACCOUNT
4. MODEM
5. NEWSGROUPS
6. DOWNLOAD
7. SERVICES
8. NETWORK

C
file of structured data = database
BBS = bulletin board system
facsimile machine = fax
FTP = file transfer protocol
sysop = system operator
kilobits per second = kbps
modem = modulator/demodulator
Internet relay chat = IRC
phone network = telephone wires

3 Word building

A

1	telegram	/ˈtelɪɡræm/	n
2	telephoto	/ˌtelɪˈfəʊtəʊ/	n
3	televise	/ˈtelɪvaɪz/	v
4	television	/ˈtelɪˌvɪʒən/	n
5	teletype	/ˈtelɪtaɪp/	n
6	teletext	/ˈtelɪtekst/	n
7	telegraph	/ˈtelɪɡrɑːf/	n, v
8	telegrapher	/tɪˈleɡrəfə/	n
9	telegraphic	/ˌtelɪˈɡræfɪk/	adj.
10	telegraphically	/ˌtelɪˈɡræfɪkli/	adv.
11	telepathy	/tɪˈlepəθi/	n
12	telepathic	/ˌtelɪˈpæθɪk/	adj.
13	telescope	/ˈtelɪskəʊp/	n
14	telescopic	/ˌtelɪˈkɒpɪk/	adj.
15	telephonist	/tɪˈlefənɪst/	n

B

1 *auto-*: autograph, autobiography, autonomy, autonomous, automobile, automation, automatic
2 *trans-*: transmission, transmit, transfer, transatlantic, transplant, transaction, transform, transformation, transfusion
3 *inter-*: international, interaction, interactive, interchange, interconnect, interdependence, interdisciplinary, intermarry, interface

4 Listening

See tapescript in panel below.

A

1 A cybercafé is a café with computers and Internet connection.
2 Access to the Web, an e-mail account, computers with CD-ROMs, games, a word processor, printing services, magazines, and the services of a traditional café (tea, coffee, snacks)

B

1 T 2 T 3 F 4 F 5 T 6 F
7 T 8 F

Tapescript

Journalist: What exactly is a cybercafé?
Daniel: Essentially it's a place where you can use computers to access the Internet. Once you've accessed the Internet, it's up to you what you do. There's a range of services that we'll allow people to use, from browsing the Web to Internet telephone.
Journalist: And what about people who need some help with using this?
Daniel: Not a problem. We always try and be available to help people if they've got problems during the day. Um, for beginners we prefer to give them a tutorial to get them going.
Journalist: And how much do you charge for using the computers?
Daniel: What most of our customers do is buy a private e-mail account from us. This costs £7 a month and gives you half price access to the machines. So what people do is pay the £7 for a month, come in ten minutes a day, it's a pound. Can't be bad.
Journalist: And what sort of people tend to come?
Daniel: We've got huge numbers of Latin American users, we've got Americans, Greeks, Russians. We pretty much cover the globe at the moment. Um, we don't tend to get that many English users. Probably because they've got access at home, but we're able to provide communication services to people that would otherwise have to make long-distance telephone calls. And we can be considerably cheaper than that.
Journalist: Is it possible to have the friendly atmosphere of a traditional café?
Daniel: I think we try to. We've had to separate out the computers from the café a little bit. So upstairs is the café area where you can sit and drink coffee and play chess and cards and backgammon and sit and chat to people. There are computers upstairs but we've moved most of them downstairs so that people can have a bit of privacy.

PHOTOCOPIABLE © Cambridge University Press 2002

Unit 28   *Internet issues*

Topics
Security and privacy on the Internet
Computer crimes
Hackers
Dangers and benefits for children

Learning objectives
To understand basic ideas related to security and privacy on the net
To discuss controversial issues on the Internet

Language
Grammar: Revision of the past simple tense
Vocabulary: *user name, password, firewall, encryption, decryption, hacker, cookies, digital certificate, filtering program*

Skills
Listening: Completing notes
Reading: Understanding general and specific information about security and privacy on the Internet and about hacking
Speaking: Discussing Internet issues: computer crime, security on the Web, personal privacy, restrictions on Internet speech
Writing: summarizing a discussion

Internet work
Netiquette

Plan

Teacher's activities	Students' activities	Comments
1 Warm-up A Ask for answers in whole-class feedback. B Direct SS' attention to the pictures and ask them to do the matching exercise. You may like to explain the meaning of key words: *Web browser, firewall, user name, password, padlock, encrypted.*	A SS try to answer the questions orally. B SS read the texts and match them with the pictures.	The Internet offers a lot of benefits, but there are risks as well. Make sure SS understand that no computer system is completely safe; computers on the Internet can be broken into by hackers and unscrupulous people. Fortunately, the net community is developing solutions to maximize protection and guarantee our right to privacy.
2 Reading A Go round and help SS with vocabulary and grammar. Draw their attention to the HELP box. B Review technical terms connected with net security.	A SS read the text to find answers to the questions. B Alone or in pairs, SS complete the sentences and the crossword.	
3 Listening Set the task and play the cassette. Check answers with the whole class. You may like to personalize the activity by asking 'Do you agree with the member of the Internet Safety Foundation about the risks of the Internet? Should Web sites rate their content?'	SS read the information in the table and look at the sample screen from Cyber Patrol. They listen and complete the table. Then they compare answers with a partner. SS listen again and check their answers.	Other filtering programs are: *CyberSitter, Internet WatchDog, Net Nanny, SurfWatch.*

Unit 28 *Internet issues*

4 Hackers! Help SS with vocabulary. Check answers with the whole class.	SS read the text to find answers to the questions.	
5 Language work: The past simple (revision) You could set this for homework.	SS rewrite the text in Task 4 in the past simple tense.	
Discussion **A** Read through the list of crimes on the Internet and encourage SS to discuss the questions in small groups. **B** Help them to write the summary.	SS discuss the questions in groups. Then they write a summary of the discussion. Finally, a spokesperson for each group presents their views to the rest of the class.	

Evaluation of the unit: ....
....

Answer key

1 Warm-up

A

1 Yes. It's difficult but it's possible for computer criminals to break into computer systems and read confidential information.
2 A hacker is someone who gains illegal (unauthorized) access to information via computer.
3 Yes. Viruses can enter your PC via e-mail attachments or when you download files from the Internet.

B
1 d   2 b   3 c   4 a

2 Reading

A

1 Because the Internet is an open system and we are exposed to hackers who break into computers for fun, to steal information or to propagate viruses. Security is vital when we want to send information such as credit card numbers.
2 They display a lock when the web page is secure and they warn you if the connection is not secure. They can also disable or delete cookies.
3 Banks use digital certificates. A popular standard is SET, or Security Electronic Transactions.
4 We can encode our e-mail using an encryption program like *Pretty Good Privacy*.
5 The most common methods to protect private networks are password access control, encryption and decryption systems, and firewalls.
6 Viruses can enter a PC through files from disks, the Internet or bulletin board systems. We have to take care when opening e-mail attachments or downloading files from the Web.

B

1 PASSWORD
2 FREEWARE
3 HACKERS
4 VIRUS
5 ENCRYPTION
6 FIREWALL
7 ATTACHMENT
8 DECRYPTION

102

3 Listening

See tapescript in panel.

1 education
2 privacy
3 pornography
4 propaganda
5 oriented
6 filtering
7 rate

4 Hackers!

1 Kevin Mitnick's most famous exploit – hacking into North American Defense Command in Colorado Springs – inspired the movie *War Games*.
2 Nicholas Whitely was arrested in 1988 in connection with virus propagation.
3 Fifteen
4 Kevin Poulsen was known as 'Dark Dante' on the networks. He was accused of the theft of US national secrets.
5 The German Chaos Computer Club
6 A computer worm called 'Code Red'.

5 Language work: The past simple (revision)

John Draper **discovered** … **generated** … **started**
Kevin Mitnick **began** …
Ian Murphy **gained** … **hacked**
IBM international network **was paralysed**
Union Bank **lost**
Nicholas Whitely **was arrested**
Fifteen-year-old hacker **cracked**
Hong Kong **introduced**
Israelis **arrested**
Kevin Poulsen **was charged** … **was accused**
German Chaos Computer Club **showed**
Computer criminals **propagated**
… attack **was launched**
Computer worm **infected**

Tapescript

Journalist: The Internet is a great resource for kids, but some parents are concerned about the presence of 'indecent' material. Can the Internet be dangerous for children?

Mrs Wilson: Well, I think the Internet brings a lot of benefits for education and entertainment, but it's not always a friendly place for children. We all have heard of things like commercial manipulation of children, invasions of privacy, child pornography, violence and neo-Nazi propaganda, and other risks.

Journalist: And what sort of precautions should parents take?

Mrs Wilson: Um, it's impossible for parents to be with their children at every moment. But there are plenty of websites oriented for children and some Internet programs can help parents to control information. But this isn't a substitute for education. It's the parents' role to make their children aware of both the benefits and dangers of the Internet.

Journalist: And what else can parents do? I mean, are there any technological solutions?

Mrs Wilson: Yes, software companies have produced Internet filtering programs like Cyber Patrol and SurfWatch that let parents block objectionable websites and restrict access to specific aspects of the Internet. Some organizations have also proposed that Web sites should rate their content with a label, from child-friendly to over-18 only. Other people think that Internet ratings are not good because they limit free expression on the Net.

Journalist: Um, I guess that's a very controversial matter. And what is your final recommendation?

Mrs Wilson: Well, in my opinion we should forget about online demons. Let's teach our children to enjoy the advantages of the Internet and to avoid the negative things.

PHOTOCOPIABLE © Cambridge University Press 2002

Unit 29 *LANs and WANs*

Topics
Networks
Worldwide communications

Learning objectives
To understand the basic ideas of a computer network
To describe the components and functions of a computer network, in oral and written form

Language
Grammar: Prepositional phrases of reference (e.g. *as for, with regard to, concerning*)
Vocabulary: *network architecture, nodes, transceiver, gateway, token, protocol, Gigabit Ethernet, fibre-optic cables,* etc.
Acronyms: *LAN, WAN, ISDN, FDDI, ADSL*

Skills
Listening: Labelling a diagram with information from the listening passage
Reading: Understanding main ideas about networks: LANs, WANs
Writing: Describing network connections
Speaking: Describing two networks connected via satellite

Optional materials
Showing SS a real local area network

Technical help is given on page 107.

Internet work
Wireless connections

Plan

Teacher's activities	Students' activities	Comments
1 Warm-up You may like to write the word *network* on the board and elicit ideas about different networks: a TV/radio network, a spy network, a telephone network, a railway network, etc. Ask SS the questions and write the definition of a computer network on the board.	SS brainstorm ideas about the term *network* and try to answer the questions.	
2 Listening Make sure SS understand two basic concepts: *local area network* and *file server*.	SS listen and label the elements of the network.	A LAN can be found in an office, bank, school, library or shopping centre.
3 Reading Make sure they understand basic concepts (*network architecture, protocol, token, gateway*). Check answers with the whole class.	SS read through the text and match the technical terms with the correct definitions.	Translating parts of the text can help SS clarify basic concepts and terminology. Encourage them to use the Glossary.
4 Language work: Prepositional phrases of 'reference' Do an example with the class to start SS off. Check answers with the whole class.	SS combine the words in the box to make phrases of reference.	

5 Writing		
Explain the diagram. Focus on the description of the office area; it will help SS describe the other areas. Go round and help them with vocabulary. You could set this task for homework.	SS look carefully at the diagram and check components and connections. Using the description of the office network as a model, SS describe the other two areas.	
6 WANs and worldwide communications		
Encourage SS to answer the questions before they read the passage.	In small groups, SS try to answer the questions without reading the passage; then they read the text and check if their answers were correct.	Most networks use telephone lines or fibre-optic cables. Today, however, some connections are wire-less (without cables). See the Infotech website.
7 Speaking		
Monitor the activity and give help where needed. Ask one or two groups to give an oral report to the class.	SS look carefully at the illustration and, in small groups, discuss the components and function of the system; then they prepare a report for the class.	

Evaluation of the unit: ....
....

Answer key

1 Warm-up

Possible answers

1 It is a system of interconnected computers that share files and other resources.
2 A network enables us to get the most from our peripherals. For example, printers, scanners, plotters and high-speed modems can be shared by a great number of users on the same network. In the same way, a network allows us to send and receive electronic messages, have access to large databases, and transfer files to and from other computers. This implies faster communications, flexible and interactive work between users, etc.

2 Listening

A See tapescript in panel on page 106.
B A LAN can be found in an office, bank, school, library, shopping centre, etc.

3 Reading

1 b   2 c   3 g   4 f   5 a   6 e   7 d

4 Language work: Prepositional phrases of 'reference'

with regard to   with reference to
in this regard   in regard to
as to   as regards
as for   on the matter of
in this respect

5 Writing

Possible descriptions

In the **engineering area**, there are several workstations running under different operating systems (UNIX, Macintosh, Digital). They all share a printer and a plotter. This area is adequate for CAD/CAM applications and can be used to generate engineering drawings and detailed graphics. The network is linked to the whole system by a gateway.

Tapescript

Small networks are called local area networks or LANs. They are groups of computers connected within a small physical area like a building or an office.

In the diagram, the central computer is a file server dedicated to managing communications and storing common files. The file server acts as a kind of traffic controller which regulates the communication between the computers and peripherals on the network. A file server usually has a large hard disk used to store common files and applications programs. The computers connected to the central computer act as clients, and are linked to a laser printer and other hardware resources. This local area network is linked to the telephone lines by a modem. This allows users to send and receive data and electronic messages to and from other computers over long distances.

PHOTOCOPIABLE © Cambridge University Press 2002

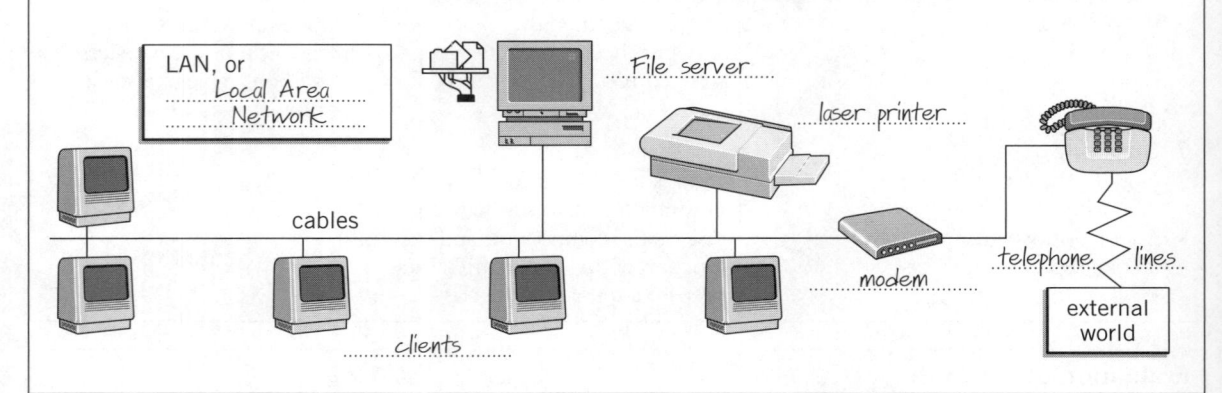

[Diagram labels: LAN, or Local Area Network; File server; laser printer; cables; clients; modem; telephone lines; external world]

In the **DTP area**, we have a LocalTalk network with various Macs sharing a laser printer, a file server and a scanner. This network is used to create corporate publications (catalogues, leaflets, reports and other materials) with high publishing standards. It is connected to the other areas by a gateway. The whole network is linked to the external world by a modem.

6 WANs and worldwide communications

1 A WAN is a wide area network. (For long-distance communications, small area networks are usually connected into a WAN.)
2 Computers can be linked over long distances by telephone lines or fibre-optic cables. They are connected to the wires by a modem.
3 Fibre-optic cables offer considerable advantages:
   • they require little physical space
   • they are safe because they don't carry electricity
   • they avoid electromagnetic interference
   • they transmit information at high speed.
4 Communications satellites receive and send signals on a transcontinental scale.

7 Speaking

Suggested answers
• This diagram represents a wide area network or WAN. Two networks are linked via satellite. One network is in **Barcelona** and consists of **a central computer and various PCs**. The other LAN is in **Los Angeles** and contains **a central computer and several clients**.
• In Los Angeles, the computers are connected to the telephone lines by **a modem**. However, in Barcelona **the network is linked to fibre-optic cables**.
• The satellite receives signals from **the dish aerials**. Then the signals are retransmitted to **workstations in Barcelona or Los Angeles**.

- The purpose of this integrated network may be **to establish communications services on a transcontinental scale**. It allows large companies and institutions to **exchange information over long distances**.

Technical help
Network topologies

There are different ways a local area network (LAN) can operate. The three most common configurations are **Token Ring**, **Bus** and **Star**.

On a **Token Ring** network, all devices (PCs, printers, file servers, etc.) are connected to the same circuit, forming a continuous loop or ring. A token – a piece of software – circulates continuously along the ring, and is read through an adaptor card in each machine as the token passes by. A computer can only send a message or document on the network if it has the token; when it has finished, it passes the token to the next device.

The limitation of a Token Ring is that only one computer may send data at a time.

A **Bus** network consists of one cable to which all the devices are connected. The two ends of the cable are not joined. Each device is able to send a message to another device when it is sure that no other signals are being transmitted. Too many messages can slow down the network speed. When two devices send messages at the same time, there is a collision and the messages need to be sent again.

In a **Star** network configuration, all devices are connected to a central station, called the star controller. The central station functions as a switching centre. Computers cannot pass messages directly to one another; instead, they have to communicate via the central station which prevents messages from colliding. This means that more than one computer can send a message at the same time.

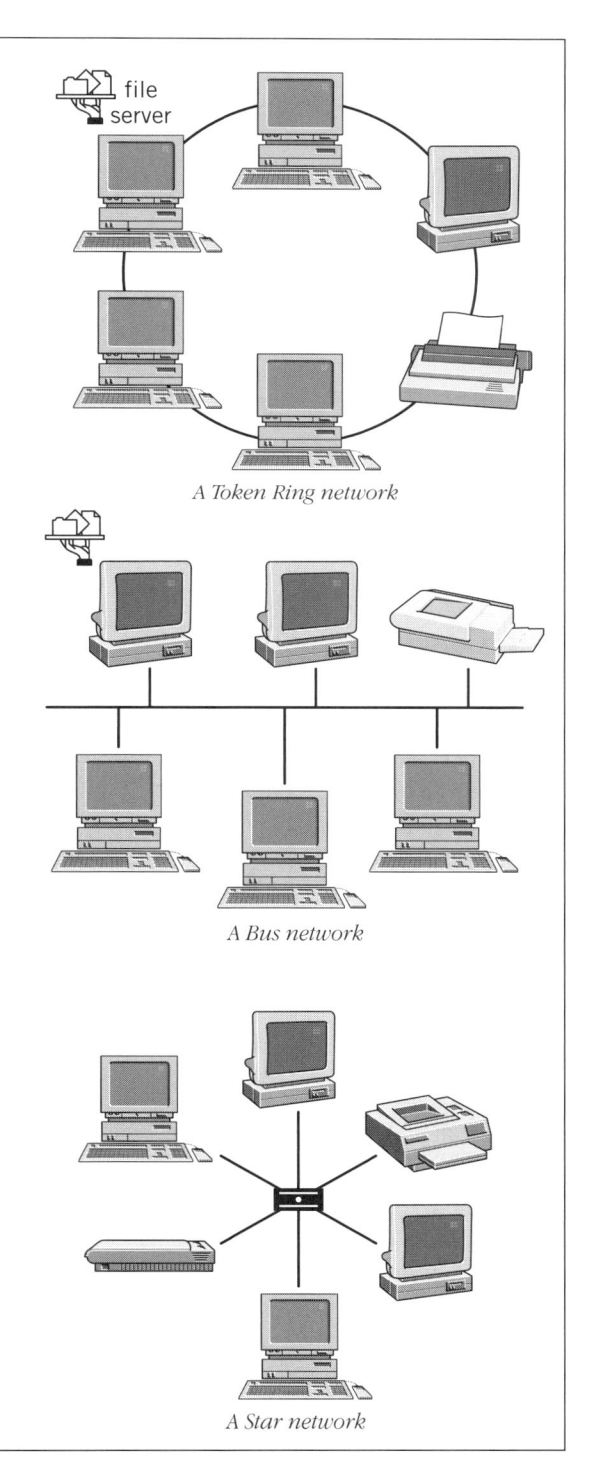

A Token Ring network

A Bus network

A Star network

Unit 30 *New technologies*

Topics
New products such as UMTS mobile phones, Internet TV, virtual reality systems, Bluetooth wireless technology, palmtops

Learning objectives
To talk and write about new computer technologies
To discuss advantages and limitations of hand held computers
To make predictions about the impact of computers on our lifestyle

Language
Grammar: Making predictions: *will/shall* + infinitive; *will be* + present participle; *will have* + past participle
Modal verbs expressing possibility: *may, might, could* + infinitive
Adverbs of probability

Vocabulary: Word fields: mobile phones (WAP, UMTS), Internet TV, virtual reality, PDAs, handheld computers

Skills
Reading: Matching texts with pictures
Understanding the main features of new technologies
Listening: Understanding specific information and language in an interview about how palmtops work
Speaking: Discussing pros and cons of handheld computers
Writing: Predicting the role of computers in the future

Internet work
The latest news

Plan

Teacher's activities	Students' activities	Comments
1 New products **A** Ask SS to read through the texts quickly in order to get a general idea of them and do the matching exercise. **B** Write their suggested captions on the board and discuss them.	**A** SS read the texts quickly for general sense and match the articles with the pictures. **B** In pairs, SS write captions for the pictures. **C** SS reread the texts and match the terms with the definitions.	Help SS with technical aspects: *wireless, SMS, WAP virtual reality* (see the Glossary). SS may like to talk about 3G mobiles and VR systems applied to video games. Spend a few minutes brainstorming ideas about it.
2 Get ready for listening Draw SS' attention to the picture and write some key words on the board: *stylus* (*electronic pen*), *thin, lightweight, batteries, PDA, handheld.* Either ask SS to write answers to the questions, alone or in pairs; then form groups so that they can share their ideas; or discuss the questions with the whole class.	Alone or in pairs, SS describe the computer in the photo and answer the questions.	
3 Listening **A** Set the task. Ask them to justify their answers or to make the necessary changes to the false statements.	**A** SS first read the statements. Then they listen and decide whether the statements are true or false.	If SS are interested in Personal Digital Assistants, you can: (i) give them a photocopy of the

B Play the relevant part of the cassette. Check answers with the whole class. C Check translations in whole-class feedback. **4 Discussion** Go round and monitor the discussion in groups. Make notes of relevant ideas on the board. (See some ideas in the Answer key.) **5 Language work: Making predictions** A Draw SS' attention to the HELP box. Check answers with the whole class. B This activity involves speaking and writing. Encourage SS to be imaginative. Check the correct use of future tenses and time expressions.	B Alone or in pairs, SS try to predict the missing words. Then they listen to part of the interview and check their answers. C SS use the context to work out appropriate equivalents in their own language. In small groups, SS discuss the questions. Then a spokesperson gives a report to the class. A SS work on their own first. Then they check answers with a partner. B In small groups, SS make predictions about the influence of computers in various environments. SS show predictions to other groups.	tapescript, (ii) bring to class some articles or advertisements from specialist magazines *or*, (iii) show them a real pen computer or a palmtop.

Evaluation of the unit: ....
....

Answer key

1 New products

A
1 b   2 c   3 a   4 d

B
Possible captions
a Virtual reality systems – a new type of interaction between humans and computers, *or* Virtual reality, a new technology with a growing number of applications.
b Mobile phones, the future of mobile computing *or* UMTS, the 3G mobile phones that can send text, voice and video.
c Internet-enabled TV sets for your living room.
d 'Bluetooth', life without cables *or* Bluetooth connects your digital devices without the use of cables.

C
1 c   2 a   3 b   4 e   5 f   6 d

2 Get ready for listening

Possible answers
1 It's very small, thin and lightweight. It's a handheld computer, also known as palmtop, pocket-size PC.
2 You use an electronic pen or stylus to write, draw and make selections on the screen. (Some models have a small keyboard or a virtual keyboard and buttons on the screen.)

3 It uses a flat liquid-crystal display (LCD). (Note: Portable computers use LCD displays; desktops use CRT screens.)
4 It runs on batteries (although it can also be connected to the mains).
5 You could take notes, store personal information, draw diagrams and make calculations. You could also access the Internet.

3 Listening

See tapescript in panel on page 111.

A
1 T   2 F   3 F   4 T
5 T   6 F   7 T
2 Palmtops have a small keyboard or a stylus (pen) to interact with a touch-sensitive screen.
3 They run Palm OS from Palm Computing or Microsoft Pocket PC OS.
6 They can transfer information to printers and PCs via cables or an infrared link. The software lets you synchronize documents with your desktop PC.

B
1 palmtops   2 handheld   3 digital
4 keyboards   5 screens   6 pen
7 systems   8 recognize   9 information
10 modem

4 Discussion

Here are some ideas
1 • Desktop PCs use CRT monitors, whereas hand-held computers use small LCD screens.
  • Hand-helds are smaller and weigh less than traditional PCs; they're pocket-size devices.
  • Traditional PCs have a standard keyboard and a mouse as input devices. Handhelds, however, have a small keyboard (about 50 keys). Some have buttons to launch programs and a touch-sensitive screen to input data with a stylus. Others offer a pen-based interface that can recognize handwritten characters.
  • Traditional PCs are more powerful than hand-helds: they have faster processors, more RAM and more storage capacity.
  • PCs are ideal for multitasking and multimedia. Palmtops are used to store personal information (schedules, addresses, etc.) or to send faxes and e-mail.
2 Advantages:
  • portable/mobile computing
  • easy-to-use software
  • can exchange data with other PCs via an infrared link
  Limitations:
  • not powerful enough to run high-demanding applications
  • limited storage capacity
  • may use batteries very quickly
3 Yes. SS should be allowed to use hand-held computers in class to take notes, make calculations or draw sketches which they can transfer to their home computers.
  No, I disagree ... / From my point of view, ...
4 I agree. We'll soon have a PDA, a phone and a PC wrapped into one hand-held device.
  No, I don't agree. Handhelds will not replace desktop PCs; they will only be used as PC companions or as personal digital assistants.

5 Language work: Making predictions

A
1 In ten years' time, a lot of people will have connected their televisions to the phone lines.
2 Portable PCs will have replaced desktop PCs in a few years' time.
3 With the help of computers doctors will have found a cure for AIDS and cancer by the year 2010.
4 By this time next year software manufacturers will have made hundreds of new programs.
5 By 2020, post offices and book shops will have disappeared.
6 By this time next year I will have bought a handheld computer.

Tapescript

Interviewer: Some portable computers are referred to as laptops and others as palmtops. Can you explain the difference?

Tom: Sure. Laptops are simply smaller versions of desktop PCs, but they can run similar applications. However, palmtops are handheld computers and weigh less than 2 pounds; they're used as PC companions or as personal digital assistants.

Interviewer: And what are the basic features of palmtops?

Tom: Well, these handheld devices run on rechargeable alkaline batteries and have small keyboards and high-contrast LCD screens. Sometimes they have buttons for launching applications and a stylus or pen, which is used for interacting with a touch-sensitive screen.

Interviewer: Do they need special operating systems?

Tom: Yes. They usually run Palm OS, from Palm Computing or Pocket PC OS, the system developed by Microsoft for mobile-computing devices. Some pen-based systems can also recognize hand-written characters and convert them into editable text.

Interviewer: Right. What sort of things can you do with handheld computers?

Tom: They're usually designed to store personal information. They have, for example, a calendar, an address book, a note pad, a calculator and a voice recorder. They may also come with a built-in modem and Internet software, which lets you send and receive e-mail from a payphone, a hotel or even a plane.

Interviewer: Really? And they are compatible with traditional PCs?

Tom: Yes, of course. They can transfer information to printers and PCs via cables or infrared link. The software lets you synchronize documents with your desktop PC.

Interviewer: And how do you see the future of palmtops? How will they develop, do you think?

Tom: Well, I think they'll become more and more popular with business executives who'll use them as a portable supplement to their desktop systems.

PHOTOCOPIABLE © Cambridge University Press 2002

Extra activities

These activities can be useful for class work, homework or self-study – in conjunction with the Students' Book.
They can also be used as tasks to test the students' progress.

Section 1   Computers today

1   Describing a diagram

Study this diagram and write a description of the components of a computer system and their functions. You can start like this:

A computer system consists of …

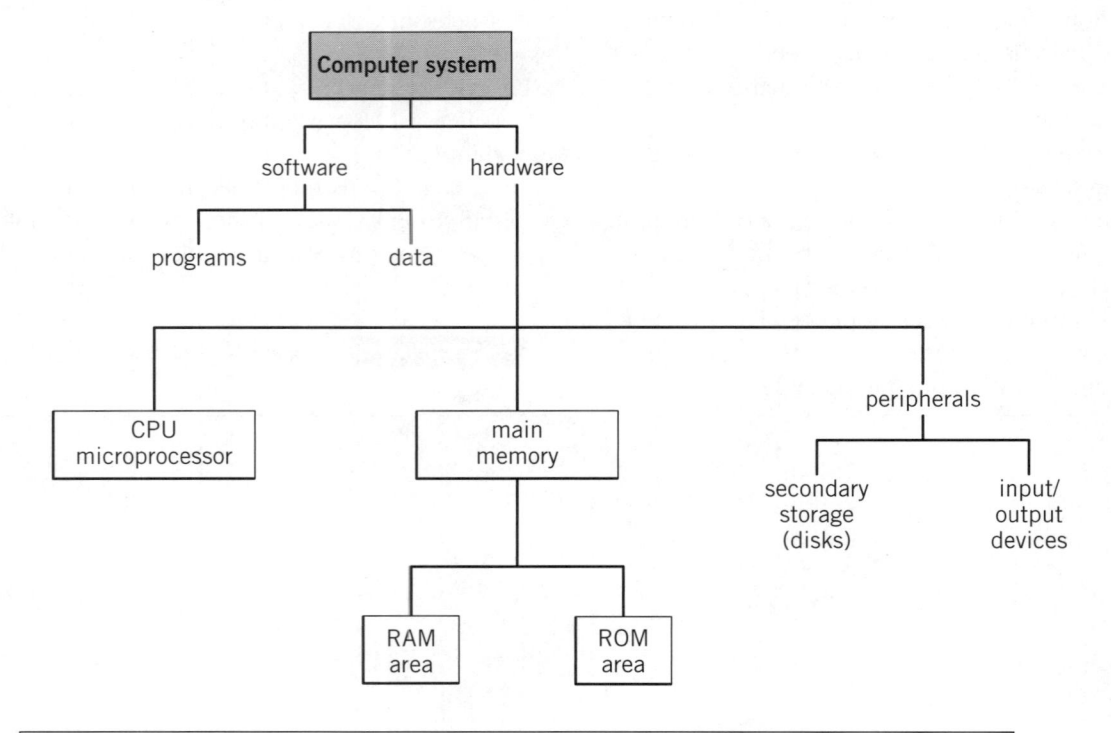

```
                        Computer system
                       /              \
                  software           hardware
                  /      \          /    |    \
              programs   data    CPU   main   peripherals
                                microproc.  memory    /        \
                                          /    \   secondary  input/
                                        RAM    ROM  storage   output
                                        area   area (disks)   devices
```

Useful constructions

- Active verbs that describe the parts of a whole: *include, contain, constitute,* e.g. *The RAM and the ROM constitute the main memory.*
- Passive constructions: *be composed of, be made up of, be loaded, be divided into, be used to,* e.g. *A basic computer system is made up of three parts: … A hard disk is used to …*
- Relative clauses: e.g. *The CPU is a chip which performs …*

2 A portable computer

A Complete the passage about a portable computer with the words in the box.

> notebooks   drive   database   colours
> memory   microphone   system   microprocessor
> menus   peripherals

The StarPC only weighs six pounds but it runs as fast as desktop computers. Its Pentium 4, 2.5 GHz (1) .... speeds through even big applications. At 9 × 11.5 × 2 inches, this new handheld computer is one of the fastest and smallest (2) .... on the market.

Its standard 40 GB hard disk is large enough to hold all the programs you're likely to need. And you also get a 3.5" internal floppy disk (3) .... and a DVD and CDRW player. Its 256 MB of (4) .... is expandable up to 1 gigabyte.

Its 14.1" TFT screen offers excellent image quality, supporting 16.7 million (5) .... at 1024 × 768 pixel resolution.

The StarPC's resident software includes a word processor, a (6) .... program and a graphics package. Its operating (7) .... is ROM-based, and shows icons, windows and pull-down (8) .... A touch pad above the keyboard acts as a mouse. There is also a built-in (9) .... to process the voice. So you can digitally record, edit and play back speech. You can also connect the StarPC to a large combination of (10) .... and network devices.

B Read the text again and complete these notes with the most relevant information.

> Dimensions: 9 × 11.5 × 2 inches
> Microprocessor: ....
> RAM: ....
> Disk drives: ....
> Hard disk: ....
> Screen: ....
> Software: ....
> Operating system: ....
> Other peripherals: ....

Extra activities

Section 2 Input/output devices

1 Output devices

A Read the descriptions and match them with the pictures.
Then label the pictures.

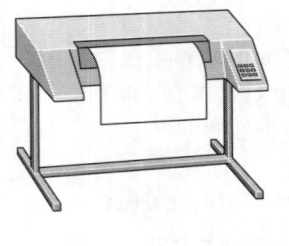

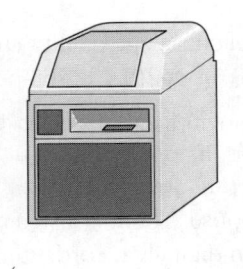

1 .... 2 ....

3 .... 4 ....

| A CRT monitor | An imagesetter (photosetter) |
| An LCD screen | A plotter |

a A television-like display with a screen that lights up where it is struck from the inside by a beam of electrons.

b A specialized printer that uses pens connected to mechanical arms to draw designs on paper. Most lines printed by this device are not built up from dots but are continuous, as if drawn by hand. It is used most often by interior decorators, engineers and architects.

c A special kind of printer that is used for the output of camera-ready artwork and negatives. It can print on either photographic paper or clear film, at resolutions between 2,000 and 3,500 dots per inch.

d A digital display made up of a liquid crystal material, polarizing filters and pieces of glass. It is used in portable computers, digital watches and calculators.

B Now translate the descriptions into your own language.

2 Writing an advertisement

Either individually or in groups, choose one product from the list below and follow the guided steps to write an advertisement for it.

Products:
- a colour scanner
- a flat screen
- a powerful mouse
- a digital camera
- a laser printer
- a voice recognition system

Write down your notes in these steps:

1 The **product** we are going to advertise is: ....
  It is used for: ....
  It is aimed at: ....
  Its advantages over rival products are: ....

2 We have chosen the following **name**: ....

3 The most suitable **medium for advertising** is:
  - television
  - radio
  - national or local papers
  - specialist magazines for computer users.

  Reasons for our choice of medium/media: ....
  Images or atmosphere that could be associated with our product: ....

4 The **slogan** for our product is: ....

Now use your notes and some persuasive vocabulary to write a complete advertisement.

Section 3 Storage devices

1 Reading

Using the text below, decide whether these statements are true (T) or false (F). Write down the part of the text that supports your answer.

1 Magneto-optical disks are not rewritable. ☐

2 Magneto-optical disks are handy for recording and transporting massive amounts of information. ☐

3 Erasable optical disks are only available in 5.25-inch size. ☐

4 An intense laser beam heats the optical disk coatings so that a magnetic head can write data. ☐

5 The data on a CD-ROM cannot be changed or 'written' to. ☐

6 Unlike conventional magnetic media, optical disks are not damaged by magnetic fields. ☐

7 Magneto-optical drives are as fast as hard drives. ☐

How a magneto-optical system works

Magneto-optical (MO) disks are erasable and transportable. They can hold large amounts of information, which makes them ideal for memory-hungry applications such as image and graphics storage, archiving, text storage and system back-up. They usually come in two formats: (i) 5.25" optical disks which are enclosed in a case similar to a cartridge and have an approximate capacity of 5.2 GB; (ii) 3.5" floptical disks which are the same size as a diskette and have a storage capacity of up to 1.3 GB.

Both formats work the same way, both requiring a magneto-optical drive. The disk surface is sensitive to both light and magnetic fields. A laser beam at high-power heats the coating so that a magnetic write head can change the magnetic field along the disk's tracks and 'write' data. When the intense laser is not active, the tracks are cool and can only be 'read' from by a weaker laser beam.

A magneto-optical system combines the technology and advantages of both conventional magnetic drives and laser-based CD-ROM. The laser used with MO drives allows data to be recorded so closely that hundreds of megabytes of information are contained on a single disk. As with magnetic drives, you can write, alter and delete your own data, avoiding the 'read only' limitation of CD-ROMs.

Erasable optical disks are not affected by magnetic fields – unless the laser is on to heat the disk surface. This means that they are secure and stable. For example, they can be transported through airport metal detectors without the data on them being damaged. They only have two disadvantages: the drives are still expensive, and they are slower than hard disks. As technology advances, the speed will probably increase to hard disk levels of performance and this type of optical disk may become the ideal medium for back-up and portable mass storage.

2 Mini-project: Writing classified ads

The 'classified ads' section of a newspaper is where you can advertise items to be bought and sold. In small groups, decide what 'real' hardware and software products you would like to sell and buy. Then prepare the advertisements including a technical description.

For sale (bargains)	Wanted
CPUs	Hardware
1	7 ....
2	8 ....
Input/output devices	9 ....
3	Software
4	10 ....
Disk drives	11 ....
5	12 ....
6	

Section 4   Basic software

1 Office automation

A Find the type of software in 1 to 5 which is used to accomplish each of the office tasks in a to e.

1 Database programs
2 Spreadsheet programs
3 Electronic mail
4 Account packages
5 Word processors

a To write letters, memos and reports.
b To exchange messages with other companies.
c To make calculations such as the tax on products, profit and loss, balance sheets, budgets, etc.
d To keep a record of employees, clients and vendors.
e To handle book-keeping and accounts: chequebook (cash, cheques, deposits), expenses (payments, discounts), income (invoices, sales analysis), inventory control, and payroll.

B Now write sentences about each type of software like this:

1 Database programs are used to keep a record of employees, clients and vendors.

C Imagine that you work in an office. Write a few lines describing the hardware and software that you would like to have at your disposal.

2 Vocabulary review: Word processing

A Some commands have been left out of the word processor menus below. Fill in the blanks with appropriate commands from this list:

Open	Save	Justify right	Spelling	Document
Paste	**Bold**	SMALL CAPS	Move (cut)	Font size
Print	Quit	Create envelopes	Show clipboard	

File	*Edit*	*Format*	*Font*	*Tools*	*Windows*
New	Undo	Character	(9)	(12)	Help
(1)	(5)	Paragraph	Times	Grammar	(14) ....
Close	Copy	Section	Roman	Thesaurus	Untitled 1
(2)	(6)	(7)	Helvetica	Hyphenation	Untitled 2
Save as …	Clear	Border	Chicago	Word count	
Delete	Select all	Header	Superscript	Sort	
Print Preview	Find …	Footer	Subscript	Calculate	
(3)	Replace …	Columns	Plain text	Repaginate	
Merge	Go to …	Tables	*Italic*	(13)	
Page setup		Justify left	(10)		
(4)		(8)	Outline		
		Justify centre	underline		
		Justify flush	(11)		
		Footnote	Shadow		

B Translate all the commands into your own language.

C Write sentences explaining the function and purpose of these writing tools.
1. Spell checker
2. Online thesaurus
3. Grammar checker

3 Computer games

A Answer these questions in small groups. Then share the information with the rest of the class.

1. How often do you play computer games? Do you play just for the fun of it?
2. What type of computer games do you prefer?
   - Adventure games (where you explore secret rooms, labyrinths, etc.)
   - Simulation games (evoking an entire world, with dangerous missions against fictitious enemies, pilots, bombers, pirates, etc.)
   - Solitaire games (where you arrange or manipulate the game pieces).
   - Games of chess, checkers, etc.
3. Describe your favourite computer game. What's the best thing about it?
4. Can computer games create addiction or dependence?

B Write a short piece (about 150 words) about the 'Advantages and disadvantages of computer games'. Here are some ideas that can help you.

Pros	Cons
Amusing, attractive	No human contact
Mental challenge	Computers don't show emotions
Imitation of real world	Addiction and dependence
Play whenever you like	Cost. Expensive hobby?

When you construct your paragraphs, try to use some 'meaning markers' from the following list:

- Introduction markers: *To begin with ...*
- Importance markers: *First and most important ..., It's essential to realize that ...*
- Linking markers: *also, moreover, similarly, furthermore, in addition, because, not only ... but also ..., on the one hand ... on the other hand ...*
- Opinion markers: *In my opinion, from my point of view*
- Conclusion and summary markers: *To sum up, therefore, in short, finally*

Section 5   Creative software

1   Vocabulary revision

A Look at the list of words and decide:
- what part of speech each word is: noun, verb, adjective or adverb
- which suffixes have been added to form a new word.

Example
designer = noun; the suffix *-er* has been added to the base form, *design* which is a verb and a noun.

1 graph   5 visual   9 engine   12 architect
2 graphic   6 visually   10 engineer   13 architecture
3 graphical   7 visualize   11 engineering   14 architectural
4 graphically   8 visualization

B Write a definition for the following terms:
1 A tool palette
2 A CAD program
3 Desktop publishing
4 Multimedia
5 MIDI capability
6 Video editing software
7 Web editor

2 Mini-project: Generating graphics

In groups, choose one of the topics below and carry out a survey among the students of your class, college or school. Then try to generate a chart on the computer showing the results.

Topics:
- How you spend your money each month
- The type of books that you read
- How you spend your free time each week

Steps:
1. Prepare the questionnaire.
2. Carry out the survey and fill in similar tables to the ones below.
3. Introduce the data into a spreadsheet capable of producing charts *or* Introduce the data into a graphics program which can convert a data file into a 2-D or 3-D graph.
4. Show the results to the rest of the class.

Monthly expenses

Items	Amount of money
Books and magazines	
Clothes	
Food	
Cinema	
CDs/cassettes	
Transport	
Sport	
Savings	
etc.	

Books people read

Type of books	Number of students
Science fiction	
Historical novels	
War novel	
Crime	
Westerns	
Horror stories	
Adventure stories	
Biographies	
Non-fiction	
Classic literature	
Romantic fiction	

Leisure activities

| Activities | Number of students related to frequency | | |
	Very often	Sometimes	Never
Playing football			
Watching television			
Going to the cinema			
Swimming			
Playing cards			
Playing sport			
Reading			
Dancing			
Housework			

Extra activities

Section 6   Programming

1   How much can you remember?

A   Match the terms on the left with their synonyms on the right.

1 program testing   a flow diagram
2 bugs   b checking a program
3 machine code   c basic instructions understood by computers
4 flowchart   d errors
5 debugging   e the writing of instructions for a computer
6 coding   f correcting mistakes in a program

B   This diagram illustrates the most important programming steps. Write a short description (about 200 words) of these steps using the diagram. Use time sequencers such as *first*, *next*, etc.

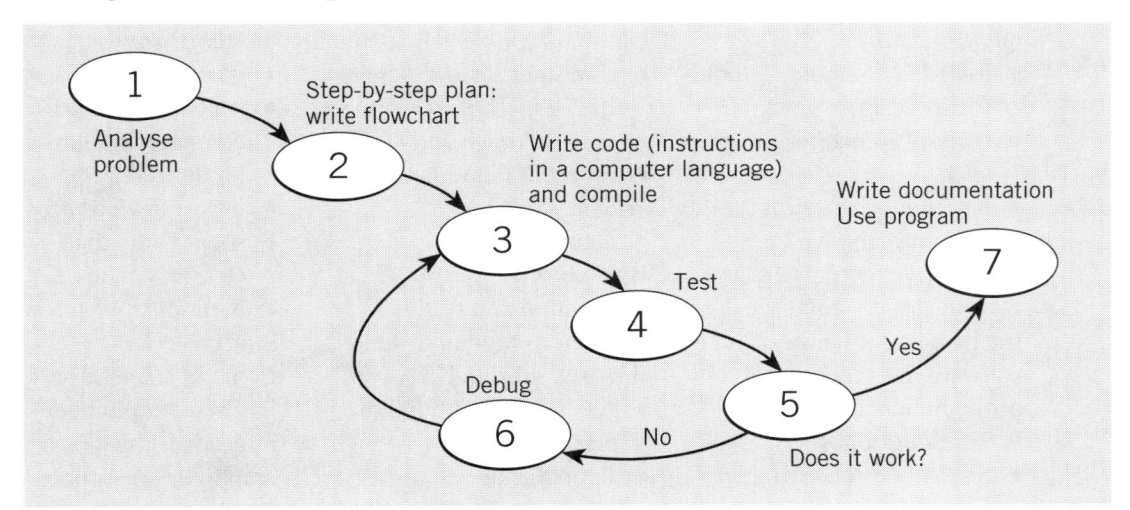

1 Analyse problem
2 Step-by-step plan: write flowchart
3 Write code (instructions in a computer language) and compile
4 Test
5 Does it work?
6 Debug
7 Write documentation / Use program

2   Speaking

A   Look at the organizational structure of this data processing department. The General Manager has just retired, so the Technical Managers have an opportunity for promotion.

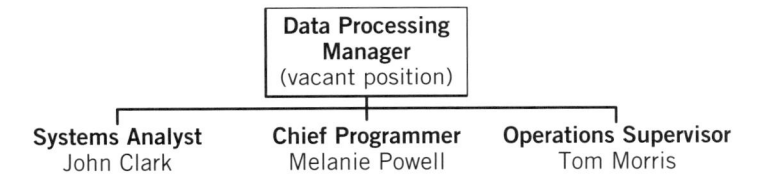

Data Processing Manager (vacant position)
— Systems Analyst: John Clark
— Chief Programmer: Melanie Powell
— Operations Supervisor: Tom Morris

In small groups, make a list of personal qualities and professional abilities that you consider valuable in a Data Processing Manager.

PHOTOCOPIABLE   © Cambridge University Press 2002

B   Who is the best candidate?

Read the personal profiles of the three candidates and in pairs discuss who is most suitable for the job. Try to come to a joint decision.

John Clark

Date of birth: 3 July 1965
Qualifications:
- followed computing studies for six years
- studied French for three years
- has been in this firm for the last ten years

Present job: Systems Analyst. Investigates systems, decides the best use of hardware and software, tells the programmers what to do.

Personal qualities:
- has a good sense of humour
- mature and imaginative

Melanie Powell

Date of birth: 21 May 1962
Qualifications:
- computer science degree 1985–90
- speaks French and German
- expert in C and Java

Present job: Chief programmer. Is responsible for the preparation and testing of computer programs.

Personal qualities:
- gets on well with junior programmers
- a good leader

Tom Morris

Date of birth: 3 June 1968
Qualifications:
- computer engineer
- wide knowledge of computer systems and hardware
- expert in word processing
- spent some time in Germany four years ago

Present job: Operations Supervisor. Controls software and hardware equipment. Supervises the jobs done by computer operators.

Personal qualities:
- hard-working

For example:

'I think … is too young to be the manager.'
'Really?'
'Yes. He is a bit inexperienced.'
'What about Melanie? She seems to be a good leader and has got management abilities.'
'Yes, but …'

C   Explain the reasons for your choice to the rest of the class.

Section 7 Computers tomorrow

1 Writing

An Intelligent Home – a futuristic fantasy, a possible reality or a danger?

Describe the house of the future in your own words.

> **Useful words**
>
> computer brain, gadgets, electronic components, room monitors, stereo, high-definition TV, security alarms, lighting, heating, energy systems, microwave ovens, gymnasium, solar panels, videophone, fax, e-mail, Internet TV, wireless connections via mobile phone

> **Making predictions**
>
> Future with *will*
> The use of adverbs: *likely, probably*
> Modal verbs: *may/might/can/could* + infinitive
> You can also describe the house by using the present simple.

Option: Imagine you live in a house controlled by a central supercomputer. What kind of conversation would you have with the supercomputer? Write it down.

2 Mini-projects: A computer network

In groups design a computer network for your college or school.
Consider the following:

- the types of computer users in the college/school (see below)
- the number of users and the purpose of the LAN
- the different network options (try and use more than one)
- whether you need access to a WAN and how you will get it
- whether you need a mainframe for accounting and data storage
- whether you need a file server/the Internet/fax and printing services.

Areas of computer use in the college/school

- Administration (administrators dealing with accounts, student registers, timetables, etc.)
- Computer studies classroom (students using hardware and software such as the operating system and applications programs)
- Departments (teachers using computers for word processing, graphics packages, databases, the Internet)
- Library (librarians using CDs, DVD-ROMs and databases)
- DTP (administrators producing material on colour printers and laser printer and scanner)

3 Computer terminology

This quiz will test your knowledge of computers as well as your vocabulary.

A   Choose the right answer: a, b, or c

1. What cursor control device is operated by rolling it across a desktop?
   a trackball   b mouse   c pointer
2. The common name for picture elements is
   a bits.   b resolution points.   c pixels.
3. Each piece of information written on a record (in a database program) is known as a
   a field.   b cell.   c layout.
4. To .... a disk is to mark tracks and sectors on its magnetic surface.
   a save   b store   c format
5. One gigabyte has
   a one thousand megabytes.   b one thousand kilobytes.
   c one million megabytes.
6. What is the only type of language that computers can understand directly?
   a human language   b BASIC   c machine code
7. Which utility is used to have a live conversation (usually typed) on the Internet?
   a FTP software   b IRC program   c Web editor
8. What name is given to the set of programs which manages and coordinates all the hardware and software?
   a system program   b operating system   c database management system
9. What type of program is used for the creation and manipulation of texts?
   a word processor   b spreadsheet   c spell checker
10. .... means moving a complete display horizontally or vertically on the screen.
    a wrapping   b indenting   c scrolling

B   The final questions

1. What is the most common graphics output device used to print engineering drawings and other detailed graphics?
2. Which data communications service is used to exchange messages between computers?
3. Combining two or more files to make a larger one is called '..............'.
4. Can you mention three different types of printers?
5. Name four programming languages.
6. Errors in programming are known as '..............'.
7. What special type of program is used to translate a high-level language program into machine code?
8. Which device is used to connect computer systems to the telephone network?
9. Give the meanings of these acronyms or abbreviations: LAN, OCR, laser, CAD, HTML.
10. What is another name for 'third generation' mobile phones?

Extra activities: Answer key

Section 1 Computers today

1 Describing a diagram

Possible answer

A computer system consists of two parts: the software and the hardware. The software includes information in the form of data and program instructions. The hardware components are the electronic and mechanical parts of the system. The basic structure of a computer system is made up of three main hardware sections: the central processing unit or CPU, the main memory and the peripherals.

The CPU is the 'brain' of the computer. It is contained on a single microprocessor chip which executes program instructions and coordinates the activities of all the other components.

The main memory is usually composed of two sections: RAM (random access memory) and ROM (read only memory). RAM is a temporary type of memory that stores data and instructions that the CPU is working with at that moment. RAM contents are lost when you turn off the computer. However, ROM is a stable, permanent type of memory that stores the information necessary to start up and operate the computer.

The peripherals are the physical units attached to the computer. They include input and output devices as well as storage devices. Input devices enable users to give information to the computer; for example, the keyboard and the mouse. Output devices allow users to get results from the computer; for example, we can see the output on the monitor or in printed form. Secondary storage devices such as floppies, hard disks, and optical disks (CD-Rewritables and DVDs) are used to store information permanently.

2 A portable computer

A

1 microprocessor   2 notebooks   3 drive   4 memory   5 colours
6 database   7 system   8 menus   9 microphone   10 peripherals

B

> Dimensions: 9 × 11.5 × 2 inches
> Microprocessor: **Pentium 4, 2.5 GHz**
> RAM: **256 MB expandable to 1 gigabyte.**
> Disk drives: **a 3.5" internal floppy disk drive and a DVD and CDRW player**
> Hard disk: **40 GB**
> Screen: **14.1" TFT, excellent image quality, 16.7 million colours, at 1,024 × 768 pixels.**
> Software: **word processor, database, graphics package**
> Operating system: **ROM-based operating system; shows icons, windows and pull-down menus**
> Other peripherals: **keyboard, touch pad as mouse, microphone**

Answer key

Section 2 Input/output devices

1 Output devices
A

1 A plotter   b
2 A CRT monitor   a
3 An LCD screen   d
4 An imagesetter   c

Section 3 Storage devices

1 Reading

1 F 'Magneto-optical disks are erasable ...' (line 1) 'As with magnetic drives, you can write, alter, and delete your own data ...' (line 27)
2 T 'They can hold large amounts of information.' (line 2)/transportable (line 2)
3 F Erasable optical disks are available in two formats: 5.25" and 3.5". (paragraph 1)
4 T 'A laser beam at high-power heats the coating so that a magnetic write head can change the magnetic field along the disk's tracks and 'write' data.' (line 14)
5 T '... avoiding the "read only" limitation of CD-ROMs.' (line 29)
6 T 'Erasable optical disks are not affected by magnetic fields.' (line 30)
7 F '... and they are slower than hard disks.' (line 37)

Section 4 Basic software

1 Office automation
A 1 d   2 c   3 b   4 e   5 a

B
2 Spreadsheet programs are used to make calculations in business.
3 Electronic mail is used to exchange messages with other companies.
4 Accounting packages are used to handle book-keeping and accounts.
5 Word processors are used to write documents: letters, memos, reports and books.

2 Vocabulary review: Word processing
A

File	*Edit*	*Format*	*Font*	*Tools*	*Windows*
(1) Open (2) Save (3) Print (4) Quit	(5) Move (cut) (6) Paste	(7) Document (8) Justify right	(9) Font size (10) **Bold** (11) SMALL CAPS	(12) Spelling (13) Create envelopes	(14) Show clipboard

C Possible answers

1 A spell checker is a utility which automatically checks and corrects spelling mistakes.
2 An online thesaurus is a dictionary which displays a list of synonyms – and sometimes antonyms – for the word to be replaced or for any lexical item that you want to look up.
3 A grammar checker is an application that attempts to check grammatical conflicts. (Grammar checkers offer advice about corrections, but they are still not a substitute for human editing.)

Section 5 Creative software

1 Vocabulary revision

A

1 graph — noun
2 graph**ic** — adj./noun
3 graph**ical** — adj.
4 graph**ically** — adverb
5 visual — adj.
6 visual**ly** — adverb
7 visual**ize** — verb
8 visual**ization** — noun
9 engine — noun
10 engin**eer** — noun
11 engineer**ing** — noun
12 architect — noun
13 architec**ture** — noun
14 architectur**al** — adj.

B Possible answers

1 A tool palette: A collection of drawing and painting tools in a package.
2 A CAD program: A category of applications used to design and develop products and buildings on a computer.
3 Desktop publishing: The use of personal computers to design and typeset books, newsletters, magazines and other printed pieces. A page-layout program is used to import text and images, combine and arrange them on the page.
4 Multimedia: This refers to those applications that combine text, sound, graphics, animation and movies on the computer screen.
   Multimedia is also defined as the integration of the existing technologies of audio, video, animation and telecommunications with traditional computing.
5 MIDI capability: 'MIDI' stands for 'Musical Instrument Digital Interface' which is a standard for formatting musical data that is understood by almost every digital musical instrument and computer music software.
6 Video editing software: It allows you to manipulate video images on a PC (e.g. cut, paste, add transitions and visual effects.)
7 Web editor: Program that allows you to create and design web pages without writing HTML commands. It's user-friendly, so you can easily insert links, pictures etc.

Section 6 Programming

1 How much can you remember?

A

1 b 2 d 3 c 4 a 5 f 6 e

Answer key

B Possible answers

To write a program, software engineers usually carry out the following steps:

First, they try to understand the problem and define the purpose of the program. Next they design a step-by-step plan of instructions. This usually takes the form of a flowchart (a diagram that uses standardized symbols showing the logical relationship between the various parts of the program).

These logical steps are then translated into instructions written in a high-level computer language (PASCAL, COBOL, C++, etc.). These computer instructions are called 'source code'. The program is then 'compiled', a process that converts the source code into machine code (binary code), the language that computers understand.

Testing programs are then run to detect errors in the program. Errors are known as 'bugs' and the process of correcting these errors is called 'debugging'. Engineers must find the origin of each error, write the correct instruction, compile the program again, and then conduct another series of tests. Debugging continues until the program runs smoothly. Finally, software developers write detailed documentation for the users. Manuals tell us how to use programs effectively.

Section 7   Computers tomorrow

1 Writing
- Direct their attention to the vocabulary and grammar hints.
- Let them decide between writing the essay or the optional activity.

3 Computer terminology

A
1 b   2 c   3 a   4 c   5 a   6 c   7 b   8 b   9 a   10 c

B
1. A plotter
2. Electronic mail (e-mail)
3. Merging
4. Dot-matrix, ink-jet, thermal method, laser, etc.
5. BASIC, Java, COBOL, Pascal, C, LISP, PROLOG, LOGO, ADA, Visual BASIC, VoiceXML, etc.
6. Bugs
7. A compiler
8. A modem
9. Local Area Network; Optical Character Recognition; Light Amplification by Stimulated Emission of Radiation; Computer-Aided Design; Hypertext Markup Language
10. UMTS mobile phones